REIMAGINATIVE
LEADERSHIP
Concepts and Applications

REIMAGINATIVE LEADERSHIP
Concepts and Applications

Canute S. Thompson

Foreword by
Hilary Beckles

The University of the West Indies Press
Mona • St Augustine • Cave Hill • Global • Five Islands

First published in Jamaica, 2024 by
The University of the West Indies Press
7A Gibraltar Hall Road,
The UWI, Mona Campus,
Kingston 7, Jamaica
www.uwipress.com

© 2024, Canute S. Thompson
ISBN: 978-976-640-948-7 (paperback)
       978-976-640-949-4 (epub)

A catalogue record of this book is available from the National Library of Jamaica.

The University of the West Indies Press has no responsibility for the persistence or accuracy of URLs for external or third-party internet websites referred to in this publication and does not guarantee that any content on such websites is, or will remain, accurate or appropriate.

Cover and Book Design by Christina Moore Fuller

Printed and Bound in the United States of America

Dedication

To all those leaders who have the courage to interrogate themselves and challenge the status quo in search of alternative ways of creating solutions to the issues that confront the organizations and societies in which they live and work, and are also willing to engage others as they reimagine new ways of living and serving.

Contents

List of Figures and Tables — ix

Foreword — xi

Acknowledgements — xv

Introduction — xvii

PART 1: SETTING THE CONTEXT — 1

1: Whither Leadership for the 21st Century — 3

2: Sources of Data — 18

PART 2: NINE CONCEPTS OF REIMAGINATIVE LEADERSHIP — 29

3: Qualities 1 and 2: Alternatives-Thinking and People Empowerment — 33

4: Quality 3: Influence versus Power — 42

5: Quality 4: Mutual Accountability — 51

6: Qualities 5 and 6: Change Catalysation and Courage — 61

7: Qualities 7, 8, and 9: Care, Justice, and Trust — 77

PART 3: APPLICATIONS OF REIMAGINATIVE LEADERSHIP QUALITIES — 91

8: Alternatives-Thinking, Trust-Building, and Risk-Taking in Two Jamaican Schools — 93

9: Solutions-Orientation, Trust, and Mutual Accountability at Jamaica Money Market Brokers Ltd — 100

10: Alternatives-Thinking, Inspiration, and Innovation at the 3M Company (USA) — 105

11:	Alternatives-Thinking, Reliance on Influence Rather Than Power, and Trust-Building in Restoring the Jamaican Economy	–	111
12:	Conclusion: Reimaginative Leadership Pre-21st Century and in the 21st Century	–	133
APPENDIX 1: Qualities of Reimaginative Leadership		–	145
APPENDIX 2: Survey Instrument		–	148
References		–	153
Index		–	165

List of Figures and Tables

Figure 2.1:	Scree Plot	– 21
Figure 2.2:	Variation Table	– 21
Figure 6.1:	Three-Fold Purpose of Constructive Subversion Dialogue	– 66
Table 2.0:	Age and Years-in-Teaching Profession Cross-tabulation	– 19
Table 2.1:	Institutional Levels at Which Participants Were Employed	– 20
Table 2.2:	First Rotated Component Matrix	– 20
Table 2.3:	Second Rotated Component Matrix	– 22
Table 2.4:	Total Variance Explained	– 24
Table 2.5:	First and Fourth Themes of Each Main Factor	– 24
Table 2.6:	Participation in Decision-Making and Influence and Advocate for Justice	– 25
Table 2.7:	Development of Leaders – Justice Advocacy	– 25
Table 2.8:	Good Listener—Demonstration of Care Correlations	– 26
Table 2.9:	Correlations among Top Four Factors	– 26

Foreword

Once in a blue moon, as the saying goes, a gift drops into one's lap. It's a mystical metaphor that speaks to a moment within one's journey when there is an alignment of reality and imaginings. When asked by the author to prepare a foreword for this seminal study on re-imaginative leadership that conceptualizes its nature at the intersection of art and science I immediately experienced the gravity of the metaphor. I had been gazing, like our writer, into this cosmos for quite some time and anticipated enlightenment to follow acceptance of the invitation.

Courage, is considered the virtue most associated with the imagination and is linked directly with the desire to lead and the trajectory of leadership. The idea, indeed, the thought, that leadership is a creature of the imagination that grows in clarity as challenges and calamities unfold in everyday life, is at once stimulating and disrupting. Creative, imaginative leadership, therefore, is as unpredictable and elusive a thing as can be thought of and is magically time specific. It therefore has to be 'reimagined' over time and be prepared ahead of its time. Timing, therefore, is the tempest and only in the imagination do we know the full truth of it.

Our author takes us with him in a deep descent into the literature of leadership discourse. Knowing fully well the tensions and turbulence of the dive, he declares an intention to raise our intellectual pulse while instigating the appetite to dive deeper. The tracks on which we travel are the "principles and practices that underpin the expressions of effective leadership". He is aware, also, that his call for us to embrace the concept of "reimaginative leadership" is outside of our specific traditional pedagogical usage and common comprehension. This is the courage that resides at the core of this work. This is the clue to the imaginative leadership he sets out to provide within the academy. He anticipates the tendency towards intellectual inertia, and he is determined to free us of it. He is an activist scholar. He goes out there, on the frontier, with imagined principles and paradigms, charting in each chapter, for this long twenty-first century the kind of leadership that "followership" will require.

In three sections this skillfully written and insightful text takes us through the origins, nature, and application of reimagined leadership as a future way of thinking and seeing and understanding for acting. It is an invitation to review and reaffirm the power of ethical and moral reasoning while partnering with the force of human agency in order to move reality and idealism along for individual empowerment and public betterment. Care and courage, he tells us, when combined with trust and accountability produce a catalytic cocktail of the critical qualities necessary for re-imaginative leadership.

The proof of the truth in the publication is found in the principles and paradigms that provide the effectiveness of the re-imagined. The leader who embraces and imbues these conceptual infrastructures manifests a quality of conduct and behaviors that in themselves represent the higher order of leadership needed for this time and the future it spawns. His thesis has deep roots in an earlier work in which he sought to locate the epicenter of effective educational leadership. It is therefore an evolved and refined construct consolidated by new research and deeper thinking.

The importance of this refreshed intervention for institutions and countries should not be minimized. It concerns the sustainability of centers of creativity and proven excellence, and emerging organizations, that are necessary to advance ecosystems in and for national development. He tells us, furthermore, that the role of leadership as an asset is more significant in developing countries than in those with long instructional traditions. The value of re-imaginative leadership in this context has a greater singular weighting.

Achieving desired development outcomes associated with right decision making at every level of management reality, and the availability of clear theoretical writing, are linked within the pedagogical imagination of our author. Again, this illustrates his conceptual courage and the academic audacity it has bred. He has emerged with this work as a re-imaginative education leader. Once in a blue moon, such a scholar erupts from the disruption of critical discourse to give us a text to set free beyond our context. This is one such moment.

Professor Sir Hilary Beckles
Vice-Chancellor, The University of the West Indies

Acknowledgements

The support of colleagues, well-wishers, and critics, known and unknown, has made this work a reality. Firstly, to commentators and critics of my previous works whose insights have served to sharpen my perspectives; secondly, to the blind peer reviewers of the manuscript whose suggestions have been exceedingly helpful.

Secondly, I wish to thank Professor Sir Hilary Beckles, Vice-Chancellor of the University of the West Indies for writing the Foreword for this book. Sir Hilary has long been a role model who has displayed inspirational, collegial, visionary, and supportive leadership globally, regionally, and as chief executive officer the University of the West Indies I am deeply honoured by the association with Sir Hilary.

I am also deeply grateful to Dr Peter Phillips, Minister of Finance in Jamaica 2012 to 2016, who shared his experiences in leading the transformation of the Jamaican economy and for having been available for an interview, the contents of which are reflected in chapter eleven. I am also grateful to Mrs Donna Scott-Mottley and Press Secretary to Prime Minister of Barbados Mia Mottley for facilitating and arranging a conversation with Prime Minister Mottley in March 2020. Unfortunately, due to the COVID-19 pandemic the follow-up interview was not possible. I am also indebted to Donna Duncan-Scott who told the story of her organization, the Jamaica Money Market Brokers Ltd, as recorded in chapter nine.

I must also express my debt of gratitude to colleagues, mentors, and enablers. These persons are too many to be listed, but I wish to mention specially: Professor Disraeli Hutton, former Director of the School of Education, UWI Mona Campus; Professor Densil Williams, Pro Vice-Chancellor for Planning, UWI; Professor Waibinte Wariboko, then Dean of the Faculty of Humanities and Education; Professor Joel Warrican, Director of the School of Education, UWI, Cave Hill Campus. I also place on record my appreciation for the encouragement and support of colleagues in the School of Education.

I wish also to thank the late Ms Pansy Benn, Ms Nickoda Worghs, Ms Allison Montgomery, and Ms Juliet Lawson who provided invaluable support in the preparation of the manuscript. Finally, I convey thanks to the team at the University of the West Indies Press for publishing this third title in as many years, and especially to the late Dr Joseph Powell, the Head of the Press and his successors Mrs Buckland and Christine Randle, as well as Ms Althea Brown and Ms Shivaun Hearne for their work in the acquisition and manuscript preparation processes.

Introduction

Leadership is an organizational asset which is deployed for the purpose of enabling an organization to achieve the goals it sets itself. The principles advanced in this book are predicated on several assumptions, chief of which are that leadership is a behaviour, not a position and secondly (and consequently) that every person in an organization can provide leadership. In these respects, then, this book posits that each member of an organization may perform leadership roles. But the book is not merely about the affirmation of the leadership roles of each member of the organization, it is more particularly an attempt to highlight the view that effective or successful organizational leadership requires approaches, grounded in given principles. The approach discussed in this book is described as *reimaginative leadership*.

The word "reimaginative" is used as an adjective and thus describes a particular form and expression of leadership. With the root being the verb, *reimagine,* the notion of reimaginative suggests action and thus positions leadership as behaviour, characterized by definable qualities (discussed below). In this regard, leadership is not viewed as a position, but as a behaviour. Reimaginative leadership is differentiated from *leadership reimagination* as the latter term, reimagination, is a noun and thus may refer to an idea like a philosophical perspective By contrast, the word *reimaginative* is an adjective and when use to qualify leadership it is describing action or behaviour. When used in this book, the construct reimaginative leadership describes a set of behaviours. The distinction being made between the noun 'reimagination' and the verb 'reimaginative' is not intended to suggest that one is superior to the other. Rather, they work in tandem. The ideas or worldviews which reflect reimagination can result in reimaginative leadership behaviours. I wish to emphasize though that leadership reimagination as expressed in ideas and philosophies is not enough. It is thus the argument of this book that it is reimaginative leadership behaviours which ultimately determine the good of organizations and societies.

It is important to assert that the reimaginative leader is not a messiah. Rather, they are a fellow traveler who acquires an interpretation of the circumstances and realities on a journey and chooses to contribute to a process, sometimes riddled in controversy and mired in complexity, to attain an end deemed collectively beneficial.

This package of behaviours is predicated on the assumption that what is stated as facts, or what is presented as the solution, or what is articulated as the only available option(s) is (are) not necessarily definitive and thus the reimaginative leader seeks to pursue a mode of engagement with such facts which are designed to challenge their state or change them. Reimaginative leadership as a way of behaving is discursive, inquisitive, disruptive, unsettled, unsettling, explorative, and prone to regard the current situations facing an organization as incomplete, imperfect, and an iteration that can be replaced and updated as new knowledge and new insights become available.

The book examines nine sets of behaviours, described as fundamentals, which are deemed to constitute reimaginative leadership. These nine fundamentals are alternatives-thinking, people empowerment, influence, mutual accountability, change catalysation, courage, care, justice, and trust.

Reimaginative Leadership as a Form of Critical Pedagogy

The notion of justice as a foundational element of critical pedagogy has been argued by Aliakbari and Faraji (2011). Reimaginative leadership is founded on the notion of justice which assumes the capacity of others in the organization and nation to contribute to desired outcomes. Aliakbari and Faraji suggest that critical pedagogy is a post-method approach to teaching and learning which stresses empowering learners to think and act critically with the aim of transforming their life conditions. Reimaginative leadership, in this regard, constitutes an application of the principles of critical pedagogy to the task of leadership.

The position of Aliakbari and Faraji was earlier articulated by Kincheloe (2005) who describes critical pedagogy as being concerned with transforming oppressive power. The views of both sets of thinkers are aligned to, and informed by, Freire (1970) who laid the foundation for the field of critical pedagogy. The essence of Freire's argument is that the European structures of education that were transplanted in politically and economically oppressed societies served to reinforce the political and economic agendas of the white hegemonic powers. Freire concluded that the realignment of power relations between the oppressor class and the oppressed, required the acquisition of critical consciousness on the part of learners.

Reimaginative leadership seeks to promote a departure from approaches to leadership which are hegemonic in substance and style, and proposes approaches which are empowering, inclusive, and welcoming of alternative perspectives. In this regard, there is openness to a wide cross section of views, and in the same way critical pedagogy emphasizes giving space to the learner for questioning, rebutting, doubting, and framing a new world view, reimaginative leadership encourages questioning, doubting, and rebutting, as solutions are sought. This can be a messy affair.

Beckett et al. (2012) expand to notion of critical pedagogy to the practice of community-building. The underlying principle which informs their argument is that the transformation of spaces in which people live is the ultimate purpose of learning. The upshot of this view is that improving the quality of life in community requires the input of all. This conclusion is consistent with the shared-leadership notion of reimaginative leadership.

The book explores principles and practices of reimaginative leadership. The word principle is used to describe a set of propositions which are being set forth as a foundational starting point or framework for a set of behaviours. These behaviours are expressed in this book as a set of practices which represent models of leadership behaviours. Reimaginative leadership practices refer to models or examples of leadership behaviours. The contention of this book is that when a leader embraces the principles of reimaginative leadership, they are positioned and enabled to conduct themselves in certain kinds of ways. Using a variety of case studies, which are discussed in Part Three, the book highlights some of the outcomes of reimaginative leadership. The case studies cover school leadership, organizational leadership, and national leadership. In addition to the more extensive cases which are discussed in chapters eight to eleven, the Conclusion in chapter twelve presents snippets from the lives of six thought leaders, activists, and governmental heads drawn from the twentieth and twenty-first centuries whose philosophies of, and approach to, leadership epitomize the qualities of reimaginative leadership discussed in the book. These leaders are Karl Barth, Martin Luther King Jr, Nelson Mandela, Rosa Parks, Mia Mottley, and Jacinda Ardern.

Karl Barth was a leading revolutionary theologian of the twentieth century; Martin Luther King Jr was perhaps the leading civil rights activist of the Americas, and one of the greatest globally also of the twentieth century. He fought alongside Rosa Parks, whose refusal to leave her seat on a bus in Alabama led to a crippling strike which forced changes to several segregation laws in the American South. Nelson Mandela, also a twentieth-century figure, was the leading advocate and fighter against apartheid and became the first Black president of South Africa, after serving twenty-seven years in prison.

Mia Mottley is the first female prime minister of the island of Barbados in the Caribbean, whose analytical skill, grasp of global socio-economic issues and fearlessness has made her a world-leading advocate for justice. Jacinda Ardern is the fifty-second prime minister of New Zealand, whose management of the COVID-19 pandemic has been hailed as a model of inclusive, compassionate, and courageous leadership. Both Mottley and Ardern stand out as leaders of the twenty-first century.

A common trait of all the leaders mentioned and the features that have marked their leadership has been their courage to critically engage the existing social and political contexts in which they found themselves.

Thus, the book does not merely articulate a theory but identifies practices of leadership which reflect the themes and philosophies articulated. I sought to be deliberate in drawing on examples from various spheres of society: political leadership, organizational leadership, schools, covering local, regional, and global contexts.

Reimaginative Leadership builds on two earlier works published by the author in 2013 and 2015, respectively. In the 2013 publication entitled *Leadership Reimagination: A Primer of Principles and Practices,* I introduced some concepts which defined the fundamental elements of reimaginative leadership. In the work published in 2015, entitled *Locating the Epicentre of Effective Educational Leadership in the 21st Century,* I discuss the results of research which was used to test the concepts introduced in the earlier work in 2013. This work represents both a refining of the ideas articulated in 2013 and 2015 as well as an expansion of those ideas.

This book, then, presents an expansive discussion of nine qualities of what I describe as reimaginative leadership as well as some examples of the display, or practice, of these leadership qualities as seen in selected historical figures, world, and organizational leaders.

Positing Theory

The positioning of theory is an audacious undertaking and faces the major test of relevance and applicability. It is with this primary consideration in mind that Part Three of the book was constructed to attempt to give meaning and vitality to the theory of reimaginative leadership. Notwithstanding what may be argued to be evidence of application as found in Part Three, there is justification for a further discussion of the practice of positing theory.

Alcoff (2019) in her Foreword to Dussel's book, *Pedagogics of Liberation,* tackles the issue of the limits and dangers of theory-making, and affirms the approach of Dussel whose methodological shift to non-ideal theory stands in stark contrast to the ideal theory of philosophers such as Thomas Moore and John Rawls. Alcoff praises Dussel for his approach, noting that in constructing his theory he took into account the real-world conditions in local contexts. This approach Alcoff contends is to be preferred to that of Dussel's foils, such as Moore and Rawls, whom she claims put forth "imagined generic thought experiments unconstrained by sociological realities" (24). While the explication of theory usually precedes data presentation, designed to provide lenses through which the data are to be understood, Alcoff's argument is that some must inform the theory in the first place, nonetheless. Her critique of Moore and Rawls is that their theoretical framing are somewhat undetached from real world challenges, are predicated on ideal theory.

Thompson, Fraser-Burgess and Major (2019) engage the issue of the place of non-ideal theory in their attempts to come to terms with the realities of Caribbean society. Thompson et al. cite Mills (1997) whose grappling with the problem of the prescriptive approach of Western and Eurocentric societies, underpinned by white supremacy, posited generic frameworks and solutions for contexts and problems for which they have no first-hand knowledge. Thompson et al. argue that philosophy of education could be made more relevant to the problems being experienced by Caribbean societies, if the dominant approaches to doing philosophy of education shifted from overly theoretical ideal theory to more pragmatic and contextual non-ideal theory which takes account of the complications and differences in the societies in which the theories are expected to be applied.

The approach taken to this book is aligned to what Alcoff and Thompson et al. have argued. Account is not only taken of the differences in the realities of the various countries, contexts, and organizations, but these realities and differences have been used to shape and give flesh to the theory. In short, the underlying claim of reimaginative leadership is that those who demonstrate its qualities are successful practitioners in solving real-world problems faced by their organizations and countries, such problems for which no previous theory or guidelines exist.

Core Concepts

In examining the construct reimaginative leadership, it is necessary to discuss the demographics of the people a leader in the twenty-first century will lead. The bulk of the global population consists of what are referred to as Generation X (Gen Xers), Generation Y, (also called Millennials), and Generation Z (Gen Z). These three groups account for about seventy per cent of the global population, with Gen X at twenty per cent, Gen Y at twenty-three per cent, and Gen Z at twenty-six per cent for a total of sixty-nine per cent.

Generation X refers to people born between 1965 and 1980, Generation Y, (Millennials) refer to people born between 1980 and 2000, and Generation Z (Gen Z) are those born after 2000. Petter (2018) had reported that by 2019, millennials who accounted for the single largest share of the global population would be eclipsed by Gen Z. This is now the case with Gen Z accounting for twenty-six per cent of the global population.

The behaviour features and worldviews of millennials (Gen Y) and Gen Z are similar though there are those who argue that Gen Z are more advanced than Gen Y in several ways. These differences may be viewed not as binary opposites but on a continuum. These characteristics of Gens Y and Z bring into focus the generally documented characteristics of Gen Xers.

Many Generation Xers are in leadership positions in national governments and organizations globally, but with the advent of technology and technology-based wealth, and the adventurous nature of millennials, many also hold powerful positions in politics and have pushed out Xers from positions which some would assume belong to them. Thus, while taking account of the fact that Xers still hold leadership positions, and therefore to whom this book would be relevant, the increasing presence of millennials in leadership positions as well as the fact that they represent the largest demographic, justifies a focus on them.

Taylor and Gao (2014) of the Pew Research Centre grapple with the issue of Xers being overlooked and suggest some factors which account for this. Among the factors they reference is the fact that they are smack in the middle of the highly-talked-about Baby Boomers and the assertive millennials, both of which are much larger. But while Xers are outnumbered by boomers and millennials, the tech-savvy among them, their experience, self-confidence and sense of independence position them as voices of reason and wisdom.

Beall (2017) identifies what he describes as eight key differences between Gen Z and millennials. These differences include that Gen Z are better at multi-tasking, are more entrepreneurial, and more global. Asghar (2014) reports on a study conducted by the Gutfreund Intelligence Group which made projections about the composition of the workforce starting in 2020. According the Asghar, The Gutfreund Intelligence Group estimates that in 2020, millennials will account for almost 50 per cent of the United States workforce. In describing the characteristics of millennials, the Gutfreund group found that 64 per cent of millennials say it is a priority for them to make the world a better place, while 72 per cent would like to be their own boss. White (2014) made similar findings in relation to millennials' preferred working environment, noting that while they wish to be their own bosses they prefer to work in a team.

Both characteristics are aligned to entrepreneurship and global thinking. An important finding of this study which highlights twenty-first century characteristics of millennials, and one with which this book grapples, as a fundamental quality which should inform the art of leadership, is that millennials say that if they must work for a boss, 79 per cent of them would want that boss to serve more as a coach or mentor.

This desire of millennials may not be unique to them, and the finding may be reflecting reverberations of McGregor (1960), who advanced Theory X and Y. McGregor's theory posited that some managers had some wrong (X) notions of workers, while others had some correct (Y) notions. The X notions included that workers were lazy and had to be driven and closely supervised, while the Y notions suggested that workers desired stimulating, challenging, and fulfilling work and if provided with that kind of environment they will produce. McClelland (1967) and Herzberg (1987) made similar findings to that of McGregor. McClelland posited the idea of workers' need for affiliation, affection, and power, while Herzberg advanced the view that the things which truly motivated workers included challenging work and recognition for effort and achievement. Collectively, these theories appear to suggest that long before millennials emerged as a group to be studied, notions of work relationships and arrangements which differed from the strict boss-subordinate constructs existed. This study by the Gutfreund Intelligence (GI) Group, however, sharpens the issue.

Closely aligned to millennials' desire for a leader or supervisor who is a coach and mentor is their desire for a collaborative, rather than a competitive, work culture. The GI Group study found that 88 per cent of millennials surveyed prefer a collaborative work culture rather than a competitive one. Again, it may be argued that workers in previous generations had similar expectations but the cultural paradigms of many work organizations emphasized competition. It was not until the late 1980s to the 1990s with the emergence of the total quality paradigm that self-directed, circular work teams began to emerge in the workplace, replacing competitive silos.

The importance of collaboration as a new paradigm of work relationships has become a dominant theme in the twenty-first century. The importance of this practice has been driven not so much by a philosophy of the value of collaboration, but by the pragmatics of survival as Hecht (2013) has argued.

Thus, organizational characteristics such as mentoring, collaborating, teaming, power-sharing, have emerged as defining qualities of twenty-first century conceptions of leadership and this book seeks to explore what these and related core concepts mean. The related core concepts which are presented in this work as constituting a model of leadership, described as reimaginative leadership include, concepts such alternatives-thinking, courage, empowerment, influence, inspiration, and subversion.

What the Book Seeks to Do

The subject matter of leadership continues to receive extensive coverage in books that seek to prepare people for responsibility in organizations and keep them updated on new research and conversations. This work offers a perspective on leadership which emphasizes the importance of the core concepts of leadership and serves as a guide for engaging a philosophical and pragmatic inquiry into what those concepts are and how they may be deployed in practice.

While it is the wish that this book will stimulate extensive debate, the greater and more lasting wish is that it will lead to renewal in organizations that have had a tendency and culture of lacking the courage to engage the realities of the new expectations with which the twenty-first century employee comes to the workplace. In addition to my expectation that the book will be a useful tool in the hands of the organizational leader and manager, as well as the scholar, I hope it will also be a tool for personal and professional growth.

For whom is this book written?

The book is written for leaders in five main contexts: academia, the church, the education sector, business, and the public sector. In targeting academia, the book is intended as a resource for students in graduate studies in leadership as well as leaders in schools, colleges, and universities.

For the church, the book is intended as a discussion and leadership development tool with which the church may engage as it seeks to examine and reimagine the modes of leadership practice.

In speaking to business and public sector leaders, *Reimaginative Leadership* appeals to the young entrant to the workforce as well as the seasoned professional. In considering the probable experience of that young entrant into the workforce, this book offers advice and encouragement which invites resistance to the notion to always do as told without questioning. For the seasoned professional, the Gen Xer, whether they hold a senior position, the book invites self-criticism of years of practice and invites Xer to ponder their legacy and impact on the organization, and challenges consideration of how to create a more inclusive and egalitarian organization.

In essence, *Reimaginative Leadership* is a call to refuse being subdued into thinking that the way things are will not change. I recall being told the process by which elephants are tamed and controlled and saw in it a powerful lesson on how some organizations subdue and control its members. After the elephant is trucked – sedated – to the designated location, it is tied to a large metal post that is held into the ground by concrete. The elephant is then starved and some days later, and when it becomes hungry, it is tempted with honey coated nuts (or other foods presumably). The person feeding the elephant stays at a distance and tempts the animal with the smell of the food. As the elephant draws nearer to reach the food the teaser pulls away and pulling with all its might the poor creature, realizing it is tied, gives up. Only then the elephant is fed, literally being rewarded for giving up. This process of taking control of the elephant continues over several days until the elephant is released. Even when released, however, the animal responds on command as though it is tied. It has now been learnt that only when it yields or submits, it is rewarded.

Some leaders approach leadership in ways that are akin to how elephants are tamed. They encroach upon the independence of members of their organizations and in seeking to control and influence their thinking and behaviour, reward them when they submit. Accordingly, this book is written for the employee who is facing the threat of being required to surrender their reasoning and relative independence of thought and who finds that things go well when they simply do as they are told and does not dare to ask questions. This book seeks to affirm the need to take a critical approach to the task of being a responsible team member and while acknowledging the importance of compliance seeks to highlight the value of interrogation, debate, discussion, and sensible contrasts in positions even while seeking to find common ground and consensus as a path to meaningful engagement with the task to be done.

This book is also written for the person who aspires to lead others and to assume a senior role in the organization. This book is offered as a companion to aid thinking and preparation along a path that invites one to be willing to reflect on the type of leader one is, and the leadership qualities one possesses and to examine whether one wishes to become a different type of leader.

Reimaginative Leadership is not intended to teach the leader survival strategies of how to fit in and get by. Rather, the book is intended to bestir and inspire the questioning and critical-thinking capacities of the leader, thereby enabling them to exercise the courage and creativity to get whatever job is at hand done well. It is also intended to stimulate and promote a cultural mindset (both within organizations and society) that leans towards finding new ways and new approaches to solving the problems of power-sharing and participatory governance. The thinking that informs this book is one that is predicated on finding new ways of solving problems and posits that, inescapably, finding new ways of doing things means being critical of the status quo, including one's own habits and approaches. This is often very uncomfortable. This book contributes to addressing those problems by stimulating the conditions of organizational cultures with an acquired propensity towards courageous alternatives-thinking, the belief in the value of people empowerment, the advantages of inspiration and influence, and the will to subvert practices which are inimical to the interest of the organization. These cultural qualities create space for the generating of multiple ideas which in turn help to build the confidence of team members to be solutions-oriented rather than being good at following and remembering the practised and standardized approaches, some of which may themselves account for the challenges facing the organization. In seeking to illustrate what the foregoing concepts mean, summaries from the experience of individuals, organizations and countries in and outside of the Caribbean are presented. The breadth of the summaries is in part a testimony to the fact the book is not written for a purely Caribbean audience.

Who am I?

I am a student of history and theology. These are the two subject areas which captured my interest in high school. Within the body of knowledge of history, I have had an interest in the issues of human oppression and struggle, in politics (both within the church and in society), as well as the history of ideas and of practices about leadership. I grew up in a strong Christian tradition and was active in the church. I entered theological college at age 18 and was tutored by scholars who subscribe to a radical, versus a conservative, interpretation of scripture. One of the writers who has had a lasting and profound impact in shaping my interpretational lenses is Walter Brueggemann.

Brueggemann, a German American Old Testament scholar, has provided a compelling perspective of how to interpret the economic model and hegemonic tendencies of the West, particularly the United States of America. Brueggemann's interpretative lenses and his paradigmatic orientation focus on imagination, alternative perspectives to the dominant narratives, and subversion. Brueggemann's main audience is the church, as a community of faith, and to a lesser extent those who manage the levers of military and economic power in society, particularly western society.

In this book I am writing to a more diverse audience, namely leaders in community, the church, organizations, and the wider society, and I am indebted to Brueggemann's influence. While key concepts of this book such as alternatives-thinking and subversion reflect the footprints of Brueggemann, I have sought to re-interpret and expand their definitions, and have added other core concepts such as courage, empowerment, influence, and inspiration. Those are the lenses through which I have learnt to see relationships and thus have come to interpret and, hopefully, practise leadership.

My biases then are fashioned by those interpretive lenses, which express themselves in practice both as a leader in various contexts and as a social advocate. My biases and orientations, therefore, are pro-egalitarianism, pro-environment, pro-the underdog, pro-inclusive leadership, pro-power sharing, pro-gender neutrality and pro-community participation in governance. I am anti-fascist, anti-free reign of market forces, anti-unlimited powers over community and organization resources vested in a single individual, anti-abuse of minorities, including minorities based on class, power, and position in organization. I am thus pro-consultation, pro-mutual accountability, pro-servant-leadership, and pro-equity. I also believe in affirmative action as a means of correcting systemic inequalities and disparities in the distribution of opportunities.

Structure of the Book

The book consists of three parts and twelve chapters. Part one introduces the key concept of the book, namely, *reimaginative leadership*. Chapter two presents the data from which the insights of the books have been drawn along with a highlighting of the themes of the data. Part two explores the various elements of reimaginative leadership. In part three, which consists of five chapters, various case studies of applications of reimaginative leadership are offered. Chapter eight describes the stories of two Jamaican schools which undertook what I assess to be some excursions into reimaginative leadership, while in chapter nine, the story of a Jamaican company which has fulsomely embraced many of the principles of reimaginative leadership, is narrated by an executive of that company. Chapter ten describes the culture of an American company which has, for decades, made innovation the hallmark of its existence. In that chapter I seek to show how intricately aligned is the practice of innovation with reimaginative leadership. Chapter eleven offers some insights from the lives of seven towering global citizens whose lives reflect courage, alternatives-thinking, inspiration, and the will to subvert the status quo and Chapter twelve provides a concluding reflection.

PART ONE
Setting the Context

This book discusses leadership qualities deemed necessary for effectiveness for the twenty-first century. These qualities emerge from a construct which I have configured named reimaginative leadership. In chapter one, the roots of this conception of leadership are uncovered. As will be seen, the roots of reimaginative leadership are located in both Eastern and ancient Near Eastern as well as from twentieth century Western thought. The Eastern thought upon which the book draws are specifically the teachings of Buddha and the prophets of ancient Israel. The development of the construct of reimaginative leadership which draws on the prophets of ancient Israel are accessed through the Old Testament theologian, Walter Brueggemann. The ideas of Western thought from which the constructs of reimaginative leadership are rooted are diverse but are largely from what may be called the traditions of egalitarianism and inclusivity.

While the roots of reimaginative leadership are in religious thought, the book is not a book about religion, nor does it promote any political ideology. Rather the book is a synthesis of diverse ideas which are supported by empirical data. Chapter two provides a summary outline of data used to develop the principles in the book.

CHAPTER 1
Whither Leadership for the 21st Century

The suggestion that the twenty-first century calls for approaches to leadership which differ from previous periods in human history is grounded in several historical facts, chief of which is that people's access to information and diverse perspectives on issues is far greater now than at any other time in human history (Thompson 2019b). The immediate upshot of that fact is that workers in the twenty-first century will be generally more aware and more demanding than their counterparts of previous eras in human history. In addition to the fact that the twenty-first century is the era of the knowledge worker (Drucker 1954), the practice of oppression and repression coupled with strict role and class assignments which characterized the pre- and post-industrial era, resulted in many workers accepting their status despite remarkable protests during the period of slavery in the British West Indies as well as across Europe in the early twentieth century.

The civil rights movements which started in the USA in the 1950s and which gave birth to, and were paralleled by, similar movements in Latin America and the Caribbean, provided stimulus for the advocacy of workers in industry for new approaches to leadership. A plethora of approaches have been advanced including the Hawthorne studies in the 1930s, the Ohio, Iowa and Michigan studies in the 1940s, the needs approach theories of the 1950s and 1960s, (McGregor 1960); the servant leadership and transformational leadership approaches of the 1970s through the 1990s (Burns 1978; Herzberg 1987) and the shared leadership and total quality approach of the 1990s into the present (Spillane and Harris 2008; Scandura et al. 2011; Schriashem at al. 2012; Thompson et al. 2017; and Zenger and Folkman 2020).

Despite this wealth of perspectives on different approaches to leadership, the task this book seeks to undertake is to explore a theory of leadership which seeks to respond to what is deemed to be a somewhat different type of worker, the worker of the twenty-first century. Given the access to information which is greater in the twenty-first century than any other time in human history, the worker of the twenty-first century possesses or has access to more advanced and current knowledge. This reality informs the expectations of workers and leaders who display a degree of sensitivity to these expectations are likely to inspire and motivate workers more than those who do not.

Within the context of the apparent need for examining what approaches to leadership may be responsive to the needs and interests of the worker (and citizen) of the twenty-first century, this book undertakes an exploration of what I have unearthed as key leadership imperatives of the twenty-first century. One concedes that that art form is multifaceted and complex. Given the acknowledgement that the art of leadership is multifaceted and complex, this book does not purport to be a final and definitive statement but a contribution to a conversation. This contribution may be specifically defined as reimaginative leadership.

Reimaginative leadership is a critical twenty-first century skill. Chuang (2013) provides a cross-section of over ten skills required in the twenty-first century; these include self-awareness, respect for others, a global mindset, and engaging the support of others. All four items selected from Chuang's list are aligned with what Peters and Gitsham (2009) found in their research on developing leaders for the future. Using data from the Ashridge group, Peters and Gitsham called attention to the fact that although 76 per cent of senior executives said that leaders in their organizations need new knowledge and skills to respond to the needs of the twenty-first century, fewer than 8 per cent believe they possessed the required skills. Peters and Gitsham placed the required skills in three categories, connectedness, context, and complexity. It is in connectedness, which includes the capacity to build partnerships and nurture important relationships, that their findings are particularly aligned with Chuang.

The urgency and relevance of a conversation about the desired and required leadership skills of the twenty-first century, have been signaled by several authorities. Dike, Odiwe, and Ehujor (2015) in advancing what they call a practical approach to leadership and management in the twenty-first century, argue that twenty-first century organizations require leaders whose passion and values and approach to decision-making and problem-solving take account of the expectations of followers and focus on building relationships with said followers. A somewhat similar frame of reference was articulated by the Harvard Kennedy School in 2016 in its announcement of its new leadership programme. The five-day programme which is entitled, "Leadership in the 21st Century: Chaos, Conflict, Courage" highlights a world view that among the major issues with which leadership in the twenty-first century would have to contend with are these three Cs. The programme is presented as being different from the average leadership development programmes that focus primarily on building a distinct set of skills and tactics. The claim of the programme organizers is that by focusing on chaos, conflict, and courage the programme is seeking to push participants to reflect on their deepest assumptions and most strongly held values and encouraging them to consider how their values and beliefs may have limited them in the past.

The key issues of leadership in the twenty-first century are clustered around the component parts of the foregoing. These include the core values articulated by Chuang (2013); the skills in building relationships and respect for others as outlined by Peters and Gitsham (2009) and Dike, Odiwe, and Ehujor (2015), together with the invitation to exercise the courage to question strongly held values as promised by the new approach to leadership articulated by the Harvard School.

In addition to the features stated above, the need for reimaginative leadership is dictated by the realities of the twenty-first century which are driven by the information age. Given that information is so easily available, the control that some leaders were once able to exert over other leaders, has been significantly curtailed. The access that people have to online courses and the facility to complete higher degrees online, and research just about any issue from the comfort of one's home, make it possible for people to acquire multiple areas of expertise and to acquire informed positions on many subjects. This reality is true with respect to teachers and students in the classroom, principal and teachers in the staffroom, and the CEO and their managers in the boardroom.

Given the inability of any leader to create an embargo on knowledge and the fact that fewer senior leaders can be more informed on critical subject areas than their senior counterparts, the mode of engagement best suited for the twenty-first century is collaborative, consultative, and distributed leadership. In this mode of engagement, a leader's power will be found more in their ability to organize and galvanize the troops rather than directing, instructing, and controlling them. The leader of the twenty-first century will win respect not so much based on how much they know but based on how well they are able to allow others to bring what they know to the table and to use their best judgment to inform the decisions of the organization. The wise leader in the twenty-first century will be the one who gives people the room to dream and to conceive of ways in which they can add value, rather than await the leader's instruction as to what to do next or how to solve a problem at hand.

The reimaginative mode of leadership is driven by five basic questions and explorations. These questions, in their logical sequence, are:

1. Are there other ways of being and doing?
2. What is the best or most effective, or most appropriate other way?
3. What must change for us to be our best or implement the identified better way?

4. What are the likely obstacles to achieving the desired outcome?
5. Who are the partners whose support will be critical for the desired destination?

Philosophical Roots of Reimaginative Leadership

One of the most compelling sets of philosophical underpinnings of reimaginative leadership is in the teachings of Buddhism. According to Buddha, a ruler (a leader) must first establish themselves in piety and righteousness, and avoid all the vices. Sovereignty and the rule of power are subjected to the rule of righteousness, not the rule of force. This, the teaching contends, is the ideal model of a value-based leadership. In defining the key characteristics of the leader, Buddha highlighted the following ten principles:

1. Dana = almsgiving
2. Sila = morality
3. Parricaga = unselfishness
4. Ajjava = integrity
5. Maddava = gentleness
6. Tapo = self-restraint
7. Akkhoda = non-anger
8. Avihimsa = non-violence
9. Khanti = patience
10. Avirodhana = agreeability

From this list of ten principles outlined in the teachings of Buddha, four are aligned to the core elements of reimaginative leadership and form part of the root of reimaginative leadership. These four are *Parricaga, Ajjava, Maddava* and *Khanti*. The alignment of these four principles of Buddhist teaching to reimaginative leadership, and how their logical construal as being roots thereof, will become apparent during the discussion immediately following.

Parricaga and Ajjava (Unselfishness and Integrity)

Parricaga means selflessness. The selfless leader places the organization's well-being above their own personal ambitions and interests. *Parricaga* also places the individual at the intersection of service to others. In this regard *parricaga* is akin to servant-leadership which is founded on the principle of "first to serve and then to lead". The conduct of the reimaginative leader is characterized by a focus on what they give, not what they receive. Such a leader is devoted to the service of others with an eye on what is in the long-term interest of the organization.

In Buddhist teaching *ajiva* means "not fearing some and favouring others". This principle is at the heart of what equity means. In the language of reimaginative leadership a ready synonym for equity is mutual accountability. The construct of mutual accountability is aligned to a fundamental value of healthy organizations and is often expressed in the word "equity". Mutual accountability means that the leader submits to being held accountable in the same way they seek to hold others accountable and thus will logically hold themself accountable. Any commitment to hold oneself accountable to others and to submit to the principles agreed among those whom one leads also means, as the principle of *ajjava* posits, that a leader will not encourage double standards and thus will not hold some accountable and not so the same with others.

It is worth noting that the root of the word integrity is *integrate*. A synonym for the word integrity is "sound" or "solid". Soundness, used for example in relation to the structure of a building, means that the building does not possess any structural defects that could compromise its firmness and standing. It means, for example, that the materials used in construction are completely connected (integrated) and that concrete structures are free from cracks.

The lessons here for leadership are profound, even if obvious. Lack of soundness arises when the leadership of an organization practises double standards. This occurs when the principles of leading are anti-*ajjava,* that is, when some are favoured and others disfavoured. When this kind of *dis*-integrity exists the primary aims of leadership risk being toppled for there is then a lack of soundness at the foundations. It is not integrated. Cracks exist and may be obvious. The presence of these cracks leads to loss of respect and confidence.

A key element of leading with integrity is humility. Humility does not mean that one is a push-over or that as a humble leader one lacks the power of their convictions and operates based on being all things to all people. Humility as a trait in a leader principally means that they affirm their weaknesses and shortcomings, acknowledge that they do not "know it all", is conscious that they make mistakes, and take a learning-from-error approach to life and leadership. To be able to admit error is an act of humility, and such acts of humility reinforce the fabric of the leader's total life and thus create the conditions for integrity.

Maddava and Khanti (Gentleness and Patience)

Maddava and *Khanti* collectively could be captured by the word "humility". *Maddava* means "kindness" and *khanti* means "tolerance of others' perspectives". In adopting these ways of behaving, the reimaginative leader creates a culture and an environment in which it is easier for others to say that they do not know and for them to admit that they erred because the focus is not on perfection, but on learning and growing. In simple terms, if there is need to learn and grow there can be no perfection. Knowing and affirming the need to learn and grow, on the part of self and others, is likely to express itself in gentleness towards others who stumble and err and having patience with them as they seek to draw the lessons from the situations they face. These acts of gentleness and patience do not mean accommodating indolence, sloppiness and inefficiency. Rather, it means focusing on what went wrong, what can therefore be learnt, and challenging self and others to pick up the pieces and move forward, drawing on the wisdom that the learning situation provides.

Prophetic Imagination

In addition to Buddhist thinking which provides a rootstock from which reimaginative leadership may be constructed is the concept and practice of prophetic leadership in the Judeo-Christian heritage. Brueggemann (2018) perhaps more than any other theologian of the twentieth century, has argued the case for prophetic leadership to be understood as imagination. Brueggemann sees prophetic leadership, as fundamentally embodied in the Christian Bible and continually practised by the contemporary church as being essentially an enterprise of imagination wherein the prophet, as the voice of the believing faith community, articulates an alternative view of reality which challenges the dominant hegemonic ideas of the oppressor and those who hold power.

Brueggemann explains that he was led to a wholly new understanding of theological imagination in his reading of Cavanaugh (1998), a book entitled, *Torture and Eucharist: Theology, Politics, and the Body of Christ*. In this book, Cavanaugh analyses life in Chile under Pinochet and argues that the intent of the regime was to make human community impossible in order to assert the absolute power of the state and to communicate that there were no alternatives. Imagination, according to Cavanaugh, is ultimately the cure to excruciating pain. It is the medicine that enables the suffering person to believe that something better, and something different are possible. It is that on which the citizen, faced with an oppressive tax system relies. It is the energy that leads to protest or more than just the venting of frustration, but the plodding of a path to a new future. Thus, Brueggemann concludes that if the voices of reason are to contribute meaningfully to the destabilization (not merely the disturbance) of the dominant culture, those who speak need to be possessed by a consciousness of radical alternatives.

But imagination, according to Brueggemann, is called for in contexts other than searing oppression and state abuse or other situations in which the present leadership is deemed by the led to be less than helpful in advancing a noble and uplifting agenda.

Brueggemann contends that even in contexts of prosperity, such as what prevails in the United States of America, there is need for imagination. Brueggemann is here suggesting that even in North America with all its wealth, people live in some form of oppression and an acceptance of the reality of oppressions and a boldness to tackle same is needed to redeem the American from the subtle forms of consumer and state oppression.

Brueggemann suggests that the church, as one voice of protest in American (and global) society, should be willing to confront the narratives of progress, as defined by the powerful, and articulate alternative narratives and possibilities of what a just and egalitarian society looks like. It is this narration of alternative narratives which Brueggemann calls prophetic imagination. I have therefore adopted the idea of finding alternatives to the dominant narratives as a key element of reimaginative leadership.

One of the characteristics of the consumer culture, which Brueggemann sees as underpinning the relative success of the narrative or progress articulated by the powerful, which reflects the skills of the marketers, is the fact that many consumers do not see themselves as being oppressed. It is as though their sensitivities have been dulled and they have become fully conscripted as part of the culture which is sucking their resources. But what is even more startling is the fact that some who do not have the resources to consume aspire to become nothing more than conspicuous consumers. Thus the need for an intervention that can nurture and nourish an alternative perception.

This numbness to the status quo happens in many contexts as leaders in organizations (whether schools, the school system, political parties, or the political system) accept the status quo as unchangeable and sacred. This view of the status quo leads to a permanent acceptance of things as they are and the capacity to reimagine is lost. The alert leader, like the conscious citizen, is one who refuses to accept the status quo as a given or as permanently good, and therefore boldly conceives of alternatives to what obtains.

Another element of Brueggemann's prophetic imagination is the notion of abundance. He notes that one of the contradictions of consumer society is the strange occurrence that many people in the United States of America suffer from hunger and lack of access to opportunity, despite the abundance of resources in that country. He thus contends that there is a need for a new interpretation and practice of abundance which will facilitate a new modality of caring for those in need. This idea of re-interpreting abundance may be linked to John Rawls's (1972) theory of re-distributive justice.

The Analogical Imagination and Abundance Mentality

Tracy (1981) advances what he calls *The Analogical Imagination*, which is the title of his book. While a largely theological treatise, Tracy makes a point similar to that of Brueggemann concerning the need to re-interpret how resources are viewed. Tracy conceives of the capacity to describe human community as characterized by abundance and to infuse it with what Covey (1992) characterizes as an abundance mentality. By viewing the world through lenses which lead to the acknowledgement of abundance and by acquiring an abundance mentality, leaders will be more inclined to create opportunities for others to flourish.

The abundance mentality which Covey discusses, is contrasted by a mentality of scarcity. This scarcity mentality leads others who are possessed by it to see limitations and not opportunities. Such a world view produces a lack of enthusiasm to dream and engage in problem solving. In short, people abandon the path of imagination. This loss of the spirit to dream and reimagine is often a function of the stultifying character of an organizational bureaucracy that serves the ego of a few but which, at the same time, is sacrificing efficiency, progress and renewal. Within those contexts the task of leadership is to exercise the courage to nudge and eventually overturn the systemic obstacles and free people to bring their creative energies to bear on the work of the organization.

Tracy's notion of analogical imagination is traceable to his Aristotelian roots as a student of Aristotelian logic. Aristotle was himself influenced by Socrates who had declared that the "unexamined life is not worth living". The process of examination invites us to imagine. Tracy posits that the power of analogical imagination is to spot the similar in the dissimilar thus analogical imagination at work in systematic theology is free to note the profound similarity in difference of all reality. Ultimately the use of analogical imagination invites wonder and amazement as those who engage in it are prone to open themselves to uncharted and unexpected paths of possibility. Through analogical imagination we can believe that what we thought impossible is possible, not only as a dialogical construct, but by examining the real world of others who have created value and life-saving outcomes in the context of their peculiar reality.

Analogical imagination asserts that amazement about another's reality challenges us to reimagine our own reality in ways that mirror the wonder and amazement that we have seen. In business parlance this is referred to as benchmarking. Benchmarking is a process of measuring an organization's internal processes and then looking across one's industry as well as other industries to identify and understand successful practices of other organizations. This is done to see which of those internal and external industry practices may be adopted from other organizations considered to be best-in-class. As such analogical imagination, but more so reimagination, is more than benchmarking. Benchmarking then seeks to identify what is. Reimagination on the other hand looks at what is and conceives of higher forms of what may be possible. Analogical imagination, therefore, provides a basis for embarking on a more courageous undertaking of reimagining and reconstructing one's reality.

Reimaginative Leadership as Responsiveness and Radicalism

The leadership style of former US President Donald Trump have forced a consideration of whether the canons of leadership which are built on concepts such as service, trust, care for others, truthfulness, have been abolished for good. With the rise of Trump to the presidency of the United States, despite not having any public service experience and with a questionable business record which has been dotted by several bankruptcies, plus the kind of crude and unlawful approaches which his former lawyer Michael Cohen (2020) has adumbrated, raises the question whether the standards of leadership have changed. Much of what Cohen has disclosed in his book was part of public conversation ahead of the 2016 General Elections. That fact makes the question of the things for which citizens look in selecting leaders even more relevant.

One of the explanations advanced for Trump's election is that he played to people's fears and sought to convey that he understood what they were experiencing. This increased his likeability.

Lebowitz (2017) discusses "16 Psychological Tricks to make people like us immediately". The first and the last on this list are: (1) copy the people you are with, and (2) act like you like them. Seidman (2018) supports Lebowitz, arguing that likability is a function of perception that the other person is like us. Seidman cautions, however, that the research shows that there is a difference between having a lot in common with someone and believing that we have a lot in common with them. Thus, in the context of politics, there is a difference between causing people to believe we have a lot in common with them and having a lot in common. But the successful politician is likely to be one who can convince citizens that they are like them.

The factors which drive likeability may be described as responsiveness factors. Being responsive means understanding the issues people face and when responses are made the leader is liked for their responsiveness. Arguably, therefore, that one element of reimaginative leadership is being able to get in touch with how people feel. Goleman (1998) describes this as emotional intelligence. Responsiveness, however, though important, is not enough if a leader is going to leave a reimaginative and transformative record. They will have to be radical and move beyond the self-serving expectations of likers to imagine what will serve a larger and longer-term agenda. Likers' tastes go and come as likers go and come, it is impossible to build a society around the transient expectations of likers. The capacity to imagine a society that is not hostage to the present expectations of likers and articulate a vision of what that society may look like and share that vision with both likers and non-likers and win support for a transformative and reimaginative agenda is, what makes the reimaginative leader stand out from other leaders. The burning question is: How?

The discourse of this book addresses the question of "how" and represents a critique of approaches to leadership which are rooted in, or informed by, worldviews which emphasize likeability as an alternative to visionary engagement. The important task of leadership responsiveness must be matched by visionary radicalism rooted in the will to challenge the self and others to rise to a higher level.

Reimaginative Leadership as a Literary Construct

The prefix "re" in the word *reimaginative* is significant and carries three distinct meanings. In the first place, it is intended to be synonymous with the "re" in the word "research" which means "again". In this regard, the posture of reimaginative leadership is a proposition that whatever undertakings an organization has pursued, and in relation to which it has been successful, there are new ways it may see and undertake such, and similar undertakings. Thus, in the mind of the reimaginative leader, there is always room for re-visiting, re-viewing, re-examining, and re-thinking.

A second meaning of the prefix "re" is a historicist's invitation to reflect on the past. In this vein, the craft of reimaginative leadership may be seen in parallel to the Enlightenment. The Enlightenment was characterized by a "discovery", upon which the then thinkers and shapers of thought came. This "discovery" was that in order to understand, influence, and shape society they needed to re-turn to ancient teachings and ideas, and from these draw new insights and inspiration for their time. In a similar manner, this burgeoning discipline of reimaginative leadership as espoused in this book, is a call to re-turn to ancient and not-so-ancient epiphanies as we seek to make sense of the dilemmas, contradictions, ambiguities, opportunities and demands of our time.

Yet another meaning that the "re" in *reimaginative* is intended to convey in some form, is a deference to the work of Walter Brueggemann whose classical and seminal works, particularly *The Prophetic Imagination,* have influenced my thinking. In *The Prophetic Imagination,* Brueggemann argues that an authentic assumption of the role of prophet, places one is a position in which they must exercise the courage to imagine and articulate a world view that stands in contrast to the dominant (or royal) world view. This perspective on the notion of courage represents, in my view, the most compelling definition of the word 'courage'. Courage is the capacity and willingness to imagine and articulate, when necessary, a perspective which stands in contrast to the dominant perspective and the determination to stand by that perspective regardless of the cost.

The dominant world view is predicated on power and control and advances a narrative that serves the interests of the powerful. Prophetic imagination challenges that world view and advances an alternative view of reality that contradicts the claims of the palace (seat of power) and in that daring contradiction of the powerful gives hope and inspiration to those who have been bruised and chastened by the effects of the narrative of the powerful.

It is to be readily acknowledged, however, that it is equally an act of courage, but also one of commonsense and wisdom for a person to reverse themselves on a stance taken when data or later discovered facts warrant a review of one's position. Maintaining a previously held position in the face of facts which disconfirm one's position is in fact as act of folly.

Summary

The critical contextual assumption and position of this work is that leadership in the twenty-first century needs to be different than what it has been in previous eras. Two principal considerations have informed the determination that a new approach to leadership is needed in the twenty-first century. The first consideration is that the twenty-first century is characterized by features which are unique to it, particularly the access to information. This condition means that citizens or workers have a greater likelihood of being informed on issues of interest as knowledge is a commodity. The fact of being more informed means that there is a strong likelihood of increased demand for attention and for one's perspectives to be heard.

The second consideration is that there is an emerging view, as articulated by the respected Harvard Kennedy School, and others, that leadership in the twenty-first century needs to be different from what leadership was in previous eras. This book articulates what the shape of that new leadership approach could be. The book is also informed by two basic assumptions namely that leadership is a behaviour, not a position and secondly, that every person in an organization can provide leadership. The book, therefore, promotes an ideology of what Spillane and Harris (2008) describe as shared leadership.

While reimaginative leadership is to some extent about shared leadership, it is more than just shared leadership. It is leadership characterized by alternatives-thinking, compassion, courage, egalitarianism, equity, humility, and mutual accountability. It is these qualities which distinguish reimaginative leadership from other forms of, or approaches to, leadership. These characterizations of leadership have been informed largely by Eastern thinking such as the teachings of Buddha and Judeo-Christianity, as well as some Western thinkers and the findings of primary research conducted by the author and other global research. The claim of this book is that reimaginative leadership embodies the approaches to leadership which are vital, and necessary for leading in the context of the twenty-first century and constitute a disposition to challenge the status quo and articulate a vision of a radically different and better organization or society.

CHAPTER 2
Sources of Data

The data which inform this book are a mix of both primary and secondary sources, which were largely quantitative in nature. The limited amount of qualitative data was gleaned from the secondary sources accessed. The primary data were drawn from two sources. The principal source of primary data was a quantitative study which involved a survey among ninety-seven teachers in Jamaica. The survey was conducted between 2013 and 2014 using a convenience sampling technique. The use of convenience sampling was the preferred method given the ease of access to members of the target population. The sample consisted of teachers from all four levels of the education system, early childhood through to tertiary. The particular sector of the tertiary system which was targeted was community colleges. The survey consisted of twenty male and seventy-seven female teachers and was conducted to ascertain teachers' perspectives on various leadership constructs and principles. In Jamaica, males account for about twenty-five per cent of the teaching force and thus a twenty per cent representation in this sample was adequate.

In deciding on the constructs to explore, I drew on my interactions with teachers over several years as well as perspectives in the literature on shared leadership and subversive thinking. These items, therefore, reflected the embodiment of my personal leadership ideologies and philosophical leanings and the zone within which I sought to make my contribution to the debate on leadership. The items reflected constructs such as power-sharing, listening, attitudes to accepting correction when errors are made, ethics of care, decision-making approaches, and people development practices and philosophies. The instrument was tested for internal consistency using Cronbach's alpha. The test generated a result of 0.938 which exceeded the ideal standard of 0.90 advanced by Nunnally (1978).

The data show, as evidenced in table 2.0, that almost sixty per cent of the participants in the survey were in the age cohorts of twenty to thirty and thirty-one to forty years old and thus, for the most part would be classifiable as millennials.

Table 2.0: Age and Years-in-Teaching Profession Cross-tabulation

		5 years or less	6–10 years	11–15 years	16–20 years	Over 20 years	Total
Age Group	20–30 years	8	5	0	0	0	13
	31–40 years	12	15	13	5	0	45
	41–50 years	2	1	7	4	6	20
	51–60 years	0	0	0	2	12	14
	60 + years	0	0	0	1	2	3
	Blank	0	0	0	0	0	2
Total		22	21	20	12	20	97

The key elements of the data which have been extracted, using SPSS V 19, are as follows in table 2.1.

The data were run through two rounds of rotated component matrix. The first round produced two top factors, namely "Demonstrate care" and "Interest in the Opinions of Staff' as in table 2.2. This iteration produced two main factors which together were responsible for 53.35 per cent of the variation in the data as shown in figure 2.2 and as graphically represented in figure 2.1. Given the location of the third factor, "Advocate for Justice", as in table 2.2, it was considered to be an important factor together with the other two factors created, called Proposition CJC to refer to Care, Justice and Capacity. The construct "capacity" is derived from "Interest in the Opinions of Staff" which is interpreted as meaning that the opinions of staff are informed by their knowledge and abilities.

Table 2.1: Institutional Levels at Which Participants Were Employed

	Frequency	Percent	Valid Percent	Cumulative Percent
Early Childhood level	1	1.0	1.0	1.0
Primary level	29	29.9	29.9	30.9
Secondary level	10	10.3	10.3	41.2
Tertiary level	47	48.5	48.5	89.7
Other	6	6.2	6.2	95.9
Blank	4	4.1	4.1	100.0
Total	97	100.0	100.0	

Table 2.2: First Rotated Component Matrix

	Component	
	1	2
Demonstrate care	.805	.154
A good listener	.656	.117
Publicly recognize staff who produce spectacular results	.654	-.193
Allow leaders to develop at all levels in the organization	.612	.260
Seek to influence rather than use power to enforce will	.574	.454
Create conditions for staff members to participate in decision-making	.560	.518
Responds positively to staff members even when there is disagreement	.521	.278
Makes effort to keep staff motivated	.504	.446
Interest in opinions of staff	-.177	.839
Advocate for justice	.430	.688
Extraction Method: Principal Component Analysis. Rotation Method: Varimax with Kaiser Normalization.		

Sources of Data

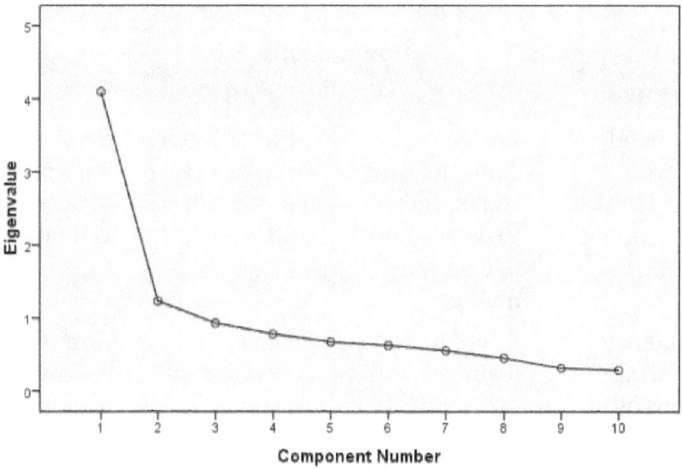

Figure 2.1: Scree Plot

Comp.	Initial Eigenvalues			Extraction Sums of Squared Loadings			Rotation Sums of Squared Loadings		
	Total	% of Variance	Cumulative %	Total	% of Variance	Cumulative %	Total	% of Variance	Cumulative %
1	4.100	41.003	41.003	4.100	41.003	41.003	3.266	32.661	32.661
2	1.235	12.352	53.355	1.235	12.352	53.355	2.069	20.694	53.355
3	.937	9.365	62.720						
4	.786	7.861	70.580						
5	.679	6.788	77.369						
6	.633	6.325	83.694						
7	.560	5.602	89.296						
8	.459	4.586	93.882						
9	.320	3.198	97.080						
10	.292	2.920	100.000						

Figure 2.2: Variation Table

A second round of analysis was done on the data using SPSS V 22 and some additional factors were shown to be responsible for the variation in the data. The rotated component matrix highlighting these factors is shown as table 2.3.

Table 2.3: Second Rotated Component Matrix

Components			
1	2	3	4
Commend staff who demonstrate commitment	Create conditions for staff members to participate in decision-making	Utilize diverse strengths of members of staff	Show willingness to accept criticism
Promote modelling of successful practice	Advocate for justice	Promote collective responsibility	Admit error when established
Encourage diversity of perspectives	Show respect	Encourage camaraderie	Respond positively to staff members even when there is disagreement
Firm with repeated failures to meet standards of excellence	Seek to influence rather than use power to enforce will	Willing to debate issues in situations where opinions differ	Demonstrate care
Make effort to keep staff motivated	Create an exciting work environment	Defer to others who may be more knowledgeable on issues	Lead in the development of the strategic plan
Trained in the fundamentals of strategic planning	Regard for professional judgement of staff members	Trust collective wisdom	

Components			
1	2	3	4
Encourage staff members to continue professional development	Allow leaders to develop at all levels in the organization	Convey by actions that others' views and approaches can be correct	
	Ensure low performing staff members receive support	Publicly recognize staff who produce spectacular results Ensure performance evaluations are done Model behaviours expected of others	

The size of each of these factors in explaining the variation in the data is shown in table 2.3.

The four main factors listed in table 2.5 – recognition, participation, diversity and openness – have been constructed into what has been called Paradigm RePaDO (Thompson 2017c). These four qualities form part of the core elements of reimaginative leadership where, among other things, recognition refers to affirming the capacity of others for greatness; participation implies empowerment; diversity suggests inclusivity and shared leadership, and openness lays the foundation for mutual accountability. The sub-factors under each of the main factors are also deeply aligned to the construct of reimaginative leadership. These constructs are explored in detail in Part Two.

Table 2.4: Total Variance Explained

Component	Initial Eigenvalues			Extraction Sums of Squared Loadings			Rotation Sums of Squared Loadings		
	Total	% of Variance	Cumulative %	Total	% of Variance	Cumulative %	Total	% of Variance	Cumulative %
1	11.68	36.522	36.522	11.68	36.522	36.522	4.836	15.113	15.113
2	2.462	7.694	44.217	2.462	7.694	44.217	4.615	14.422	29.535
3	1.813	5.665	49.882	1.813	5.665	49.882	4.324	13.514	43.049
4	1.490	4.655	54.537	1.490	4.655	54.537	3.676	11.488	54.537

Table 2.5: First and Fourth Themes of Each Main Factor

Main theme	Sub-theme 1	Sub-theme 4
Recognition	Encourage staff to continue professional development	Be firm with repeated failures to meet standards
Participation	Ensure low performing staff receive support	Seek to influence rather than use power to enforce will
Diversity	Promote collective responsibility	Defer to others who may be more knowledgeable
Openness	Convey by actions that others' approaches views can be correct	Demonstrate care

Further analyses were done on the data using Pearson's correlations and the results shown in tables 2.6 to 2.9 were found.

Table 2.6: Participation in Decision-Making and Influence and Advocate for Justice

	Create conditions for staff members to participate in decision-making	Advocate for Justice
Create conditions for staff members to participate in decision making. (Pearson Correlation Sig. (2-tailed) N	1 97	.565** .000 97
Advocate for justice Pearson Correlation Sig. (2-tailed) N	.565** .0000 97	1 97

** Correlation is significant at the 0.01 level (2-tailed).

Table 2.7: Development of Leaders – Justice Advocacy

	Allow leaders to develop at all levels in the organization	Advocate for justice
Allow leaders to develop at all levels in the organization Pearson Correlation Sig. (2-tailed) N	1 97	.405** .000 97
Advocate for justice Pearson Correlation Sig. (2-tailed) N	.405** .000 97	1 97

** Correlation is significant at the 0.01 level (2-tailed).

Table 2.8: Good Listener—Demonstration of Care Correlations

	A Good listener	Demonstrate Care
A Good Listener Pearson Correlation Sig. (2-tailed) N	1 97	.485** .000 97
Demonstrate Care Pearson Correlation Sig. (2-tailed) N	.485** .000 97	1 97

**.Correlation is significant at the 0.01 level (2-tailed).

Table 2.9: Correlations among Top Four Factors

		Factor1	Factor2	Factor3	Factor4
Factor1	Pearson Correlation	1	.635**	.609**	.589**
	Sig. (2-tailed)		.000	.000	.000
	N		97	97	97
Factor2	Pearson Correlation	.635**	1	.436**	.664**
	Sig. (2-tailed)	.000		.000	.000
	N	97		97	97
Factor3	Pearson Correlation	.609**	.436**	1	.550**
	Sig. (2-tailed)	.000	.000		.000
	N	97	97		97
Factor4	Pearson Correlation	.589**	.664**	.550**	1
	Sig. (2-tailed)	.000	.000	.000	
	N	97	97	97	

The second source of primary data was qualitative. The data were drawn from an interview conducted with Jamaica's Minister of Finance who served during the period 2012–2016. The instrument used for this interview is found in Appendix 2.

This work also relies upon two sources of secondary data, one quantitative and the other qualitative. The quantitative data come from a global study conducted by the Gutfreund Intelligence Group. This study sought to understand the perspectives and expectations of millennials and was conducted in 2013. The other source of secondary data comes from the work of Thompson, Burke, King, and Wong (2017), which relied on a qualitative study carried out between 2015 and 2016.

PART TWO
Nine Concepts of Reimaginative Leadership

In this section, nine major qualities of reimaginative leadership are examined. These qualities are alternatives-thinking, people empowerment, influence, mutual accountability, change catalysation, courage, care, justice, and trust. These qualities have been culled from, and informed by, the data analyzed and summarized in chapter two and elements of a global survey of millennials undertaken by the Gutfreund Intelligence Group. There is no claim being made that the nine qualities of reimaginative leadership discussed are the full and final list of qualities which could be ever conceived. Rather, that the foundational framework of reimaginative leadership is embodied in these nine qualities.

Chapter three examines alternatives-thinking and people empowerment. The relationship between these two qualities and their location in the sequence of the nine qualities are critical to understanding them and their relationship to the other qualities. "Alternatives-thinking" is the base of reimaginative leadership (Brueggemann [1978] posits it as the heart of prophetic imagination). The alternatives-thinking leader is one who is not held hostage by the prevailing circumstances or practices and is willing to propose and posit world views which are at odds with the dominant narratives and prevailing expectations. Similarly, an astute leader recognizes that the ultimate measure of their effectiveness is found in the quality and quantity of leaders they develop. The best strategy for developing leaders is empowering people. Thus, it is through modelling (Thompson 2019b) that the leader empowers. In this regard an alternatives-thinking leader empowers those they lead to engage in alternatives-thinking.

Chapter four discusses the third quality of reimaginative leadership – influence – and contrasts it with its opposite quality, power. The word power is used here to refer to force, pressure, raw executive authority, and coercion. The contention here is that the source of creative ideation is not pressure placed on individuals through executive authority, coercion, instruction, and direction but influence, motivation, and inspiration. Following from the foundational qualities of alternatives-thinking and empowerment, the location of influence in the pantheon of twenty-first century leadership qualities suggests that once a leader empowers people they "authorize" them to question and talk back, thus the nature of the process of engagement in the pursuit of organizational goals is not about edicts and directives but conversation compromise, shared ideas with the leader using their capacity to persuade and to inspire, to influence behaviour as may be required from time to time.

The preference for influence over instruction and coercion (power) as the mode of reimaginative leadership is further explained in chapter five where the construct of mutual accountability is discussed. Traditional notions of accountability posit that the person in a position of superior power holds those with less or no power accountable. Reimaginative leadership rejects this notion and posits instead the construct of *mutual* accountability. Mutual accountability occurs when those who seek to hold others accountable recognize that they too are accountable and submit themselves to be held accountable by those they lead (Thompson 2018e).

Having established alternatives-thinking as the basis of reimaginative leadership which then leads to empowerment, and further requires leadership by inspiration rather than instruction, thus producing a culture of mutuality in accountability, the organization is positioned for real change. Another way of expressing this idea is that change becomes possible, and when it occurs it is likely to be more sustainable, when employees are empowered, when leadership leverages influence rather than power, and when there is equity in accountability. The processes for catalysing change, which will invariably require courage, are discussed in chapter six. Change catalysation and courage represent the fifth and sixth of the nine twenty-first century leadership qualities advanced in this book.

The qualities of care, justice, and trust round out the nine qualities. These qualities represent the personality and passion of reimaginative leadership. As discussed in chapter seven, care and justice involve, among other things, disciplined efforts through policy and practice to give employees a space to be heard. So, while alternatives-thinking and empowerment represent the ideological grounding of reimaginative leadership, care and justice constitute the visible application. The credibility of the efforts to show care and deliver justice is hinged on creating the environment for trust which depends on the expression of specific leadership behaviours (Thompson 2018a).

CHAPTER 3
Qualities 1 and 2: Alternatives-Thinking and People Empowerment

In table 2.2, it was shown that one sub-factor of the factor "Demonstrating care" was "responding positively when there is disagreement". The existence of disagreement suggests that the parties have expressed different points of view. This difference of points of view, extracted from the context, is expected of a leader: it highlights the need for a leader to be open to alternative points of view.

A second sub-factor in table 2.2 which is aligned to the topic of this chapter is the issue of the expectation that the leader of the organization will facilitate the development of leaders "at all levels in the organization". This finding is supported by the finding in table 2.5 which shows a moderate correlation of .405 between the variables "allows leaders to develop at all levels of the organization" and "advocate for justice". These findings, taken together, suggest that among the elements of the art of leadership in the twenty-first century, are behaviours which support disagreement and promote the development of leadership, with the latter being seen as a justice issue.

The act of reimagining inescapably involves taking a discordant view of what is striving for a new perspective or approach. In this regard, reimaginative leadership is a discipline in *alternatives-thinking*. Alternatives-thinking is basically the belief that there are probably smarter, more efficient, more inclusive, more effective, more people-oriented, more customer-service driven ways of conducting business. Alternatives-thinking assumes that there are good ways of getting things done but is characterized by an inclination to wonder aloud whether there may not be a better way.

Thus, in this mode of thinking, the leader is prepared to critique the status quo. Reimaginative leadership as a mode of operating, contends that the critique of the status quo is predicated on the belief that the organization or community can, through the process of reflection and conversation, arrive at a better place.

There is an interesting story of a meeting of the top management team at General Motors. It is said that at the end of a meeting Alfred Sloan, the CEO said, "Gentlemen, I take it we are all in complete agreement on the decision here?" All the managers around the table nodded in agreement. Sloan then continued, "Then, I propose we postpone further discussion of this matter until our next meeting to give ourselves time to develop disagreement and perhaps gain some understanding of what this decision is about."

It is the proposition of this book that self-criticism as a mode of (both personal and organizational) existence is being increasingly demanded in the twenty-first century. Several considerations support this. One is the fact that, as many studies have shown, greater and more value-added ideas come out of a process of interrogation and debate. But the other important consideration is the fact that the expectation of workers in this generation is that they be consulted. Thus, if the general managers were to adopt Alfred Sloan's approach, they would find that there would not be nods all around.

The worker of the twenty-first century lives in an era in which knowledge is a commodity and "information supermarkets" are always open. The online reality of the twenty-first century with automatic access to information alters the power dynamic of relationships, given that knowledge is power. The implications of the age of the commoditization of knowledge are many, two of which are that it is now very difficult to keep workers in the dark and every worker can develop *expertise*. The existence of the resources for the acquisition of expertise means that we are in an era called the *end of expertise*. There are voluminous sources of do-it-yourself and the internet makes it possible for functions which were once done by experts at an office, to be done from the comfort of one's home. These include online banking, airline reservations, diagnoses of causes of certain illnesses. With these advances, many jobs as we know them no longer exist and these are being replaced by other types of jobs that were hitherto unknown. The emergence of artificial intelligence has made this reality even more daunting.

Reimaginative Leadership as People Empowerment

With alternatives-thinking being the fundamental quality of reimaginative leadership, there is an inherent assumption that if alternatives-thinking is embraced then the organization must simultaneously give space and power for people to imagine, for people to "think outside the box", for people to wonder aloud, for people to ask "why"? People empowerment is not achieved merely by establishing structures that provide for more persons to occupy "management" positions. People empowerment begins with the creation and fostering of a culture that encourages differences of opinion, nurtures intellectual diversity, and rewards those who are bold and daring enough to produce superior results without being slaves to the existing paths, provided the paths they take are both legal and ethical.

The notion of diversity, as defined in the data presented in chapter two and elaborated in Paradigm RePaDO (Thompson 2017c) is embedded in the idea that members of an organization bring different gifts and abilities to the workplace. The task of leadership in this regard is that of creating the space, through organizational culture, policies, and practices, for employees to bring their talents to the fore in impacting the work of the organization. In this regard, the embrace of diversity and the facilitation of its expression are connected to the principle of participation (the 'Pa' in RePaDO).

An approach to organizational leadership which is informed by the embrace of diversity will take account not only of the documented, formal, and specialized training and skills which employees possess, but also those creative and peculiar skills and interests which help to define their personalities and propensities. The task of leadership, in managing this kind of diversity, requires imagination and patience in allowing for the experimentation and learning-from-errors mindset in order to allow the organization to benefit from the diverse talents of employees. This approach to leadership is largely what empowerment means. Authentic people empowerment, which often expresses itself in rewarding those who achieve spectacular results outside the regular paths, does not mean that when spectacular results are not immediately forthcoming, or when there are errors, people are ignored or punished. A people-empowering culture in fact gives space for people to err and encourages learning from errors.

The renowned leadership authority, Kotter (2013) contends that leadership is about taking an organization into the future and posits that ultimately it is about vision, about people buying in, about empowerment and successful change. When thus positioned, leadership involves, he says, finding opportunities that are coming at the organization faster and faster and exploiting these opportunities. I suggest, however, that leadership is more critically about successfully *creating* (not just finding) opportunities at a rapid rate and in so doing locating the organization at a place in the present and the future where it can stand tall among its competitors. A good example of this kind of leadership is the company IBM. IBM was once known mainly for servers and hardware and when it faced competition from new market entrants such as Apple and Microsoft there was the emerging narrative that IBM would go out of business. But consistent with the philosophy of creating opportunities, IBM repositioned itself and is once again a major industry player in a variety of areas in the information technology field. A report by Boyden World Corporation highlights that for 2018 IBM would be "targeting annual revenues of around $40 billion, which would come from areas hitherto virtually unknown. These included cloud computing, big data, security software, analytics, mobile, and social".

The art of successfully creating opportunities will be fuelled by the capacity of organizations to be disruptive in their innovative capacities as well as to respond quickly to trends in disruptive innovation. According to Anthony (2013), whereas in an earlier era organizational leaders may have had the luxury of holding onto their market share with the products and services they offered, today they have no choice but to respond to disruptive innovations if the organizations are to survive as businesses. Whereas it will require management capabilities to oversee the budgeting, marketing, production and related processes to take new product ideas to the market, it requires leadership to anticipate the likely market trends and to stimulate the creativity of the workforce to conceive and design products that will meet and await the demands of the marketplace.

One of the pitfalls that leaders must avoid is that of being so passionate about their own positions and beliefs regarding their own innovative ideas, that they crowd out or stifle the creativity, passion and reimagination of others. Engagements between those who lead and those who are led, in which passion and creativity are stifled is not effective leadership. A good example of this tendency of bright "leaders" to stifle others is the late Steve Jobs. Jobs, despite being remembered by some as a great leader, was in fact a "my way or the highway" kind of person as McInerney (2011) indicates. McInerney contends that Jobs was not known for being consultative and supportive of consensus building and was the kind of leader who placed greater value on his ideas than he did on others. The tradition at Apple was that his ideas ruled and thus many of his conflicts with team members were because of his refusal to give space to other ideas. One of the real lessons of Steve Jobs's life is that the co-location of innovation and reimagination in one and the same leader, requires of such a leader an increased capacity of self-discipline and restraint to give others the space to innovate and give birth to the products of their ideas.

The damage that lack of openness to alternatives can cause was on display in 2022 in the United Kingdom during the brief leadership of Liz Truss. Truss, a Conservative in the tradition of Margaret Thatcher, implemented a slew of economic policies which sent the UK economy into a tailspin. Her decision reflected the neoliberal view that there is one, and only one, way to revive a struggling economy. This doctrine claims that there is only one way to grow an economy and that is by giving tax cuts to the wealthy, cutting spending on social services, and reducing regulations and big government. The proponents of this doctrine gave a name to this claim that there "there is no alternative". They called it TINA (Robinson 2013).

Reimaginative leadership challenges notions such as these with its alternatives-thinking paradigm. Alternatives-thinking refers to the default disposition to reject the notion that there are no alternatives and things must be done the way they have been over the years. This closed-minded thinking has been the source of substantial injustice globally, for decades.

An alternatives-thinking mindset is predicated on the assumption of the availability, or even the abundance, of ideas and alternatives. Similarly, the facilitation of the development of staff at all levels of an organization is fuelled by the belief that there are multiple opportunities for people to make leadership contributions to the organization. Reimaginative leadership assumes that there is an abundance of resources in ideas, capacities, and possibilities and thus the status quo need not be seen as permanent and as the only achievable state of existence. Covey (2004) describes the features of *scarcity mentality* and *abundance mentality*. According to Covey, most people are deeply scripted in the scarcity mentality which is characterized by a tendency to live as having only so much, as though there were only one pie out there, and if someone were to get a big piece of the pie, it would mean less for everybody else.

What is particularly punishing about this scarcity mentality is that it leads people to think and behave as though infinite resources such as praise and goodwill are in limited supply. Therefore, if someone is praised for their work, a scarcity-mentality onlooker or stakeholder will have the tendency to feel that they cannot get similar recognition, or even greater recognition. Thus, people with the scarcity mentality find it difficult to praise others and give them credit for their work. But even more troubling is that these people have a hard time being genuinely happy for the success of other people even when those successes did not depend on resources that they provided.

The abundance mentality, on the other hand, flows out of a deep inner sense of personal worth and security and what Covey calls a bone-deep conviction that there is enough of goodness and possibility all around for each to share and enjoy. The consequence of this mentality is that there is a generosity and free-spiritedness in sharing prestige, applause, decision-making, and profits. According to Covey, abundance thinking opens options and alternatives for creativity and possibility.

Abundance thinking is at the heart of reimaginative leadership. Reimaginative leadership affirms the profound capacity of the other for goodness and greatness and of almost limitless capacity that is possessed by a group of thinkers and collaborators who come together to pursue noble causes. The reimaginative thinker, who is informed by this abundance mentality, does not see obstacles but opportunities; does not see dead ends but starting points; does not say "no, we cannot" but "yes, we can". In this regard the reimaginative leader frees the people they lead to innovate, collaborate, and create and, rather than acting as a traffic cop who vets and directs, they serve as a quality assurance advisor and nurturer of talent who enriches, as much as they can, the creative undertakings of those in whose work they are privileged to make a contribution. Organizations can get leaders to this point of abundance leading by institutionalizing requirements for consultation, supporting the use of self-directed work teams and rewarding units, departments, and individuals whose actions in these areas bring results in areas such as improvements in employee satisfaction indices, reduction in waste, improvements in cost management, and increased profitability, among other areas.

Chapter two highlighted that in the second review of the data, it was found that the expectation of recognition was one of the factors which explained perspectives of teachers in relation to the ideal qualities of principals. This issue is discussed elsewhere as Paradigm RePaDo (Thompson 2017c). The importance of showing recognition in the cocktail of leadership virtues has been highlighted by Herzberg (1987) and more recently in the global study conducted by the Gutfreund Intelligence Group.

The implications of these findings suggest that the leader of the twenty-first century will require, as one of the tools for their effectiveness, the willingness and adroit capacity not merely to be generous in acknowledging the contributions of others in the organization but to discern and tap into their latent gifts and abilities and create the space for those gifts and abilities to be creatively and equitably deployed in the organization.

Making meaning of chaos

By making room for alternative ideas and empowering employees to innovate and experiment, an organization risks becoming chaotic. Reimaginative leadership is essentially a disruptive way of living and leading. This is reinforced by Margaret Wheatley whose 1999 bestseller, *Leadership and the New Science,* articulated that the view that effective leadership is inevitably disruptive – disruptive of the status quo, disruptive of inefficiency, disruptive of the practices of inequity, disruptive of injustice, and disruptive of indifference to excellence.

Wheatley affirms *chaos theory* and calls for an affirmation of the fact that nature (whether the naturalness of the universe or the natural flow of human energy in organizations) has the capacity to build new and value-added levels of order and well-being out of the chaos of seemingly random events around us. Thus, Wheatley asserts that chaos can be a pathway to order. Drawing on Wheatley, as well as Brueggemann, reimaginative leadership is a subversive activity with an important element being *constructive subversion.*

Another thinker who has advanced the idea that chaos is potentially healthy for organizations is Tom Peters. In his classic *Thriving on Chaos,* Peters makes a compelling case in support of the view that organizations that will succeed in an era of uncertainty and fluidity are those organizations that have the capacity and tenacity to make meaning of unplanned outcomes and thrive on chaos. These organizations do not resist change, they embrace and anticipate change and, by extension, these organizations do not seek to silence their members whose views may be different from top management or run counter to the majority. Instead, they see them as valuable assets whose contribution may be likened to that of white blood cells in the body. Too many white blood cells will eventually destroy the body but in the absence of white blood cells, the body's capacity to withstand infection and bounce back from illness is seriously compromised. The overarching point here is that an organization needs protagonists as well as antagonists to find optimum solutions to problems. If everyone agrees with the ideas of the boss consistently, there is a strong likelihood that team members are not being reflective enough or are being fearful which could lead to organizational malperformance.

Thriving on Chaos was first published in 1987 coincidentally at about the same time as the US stock market crash. Peters had the insight to have seen that the businesses that would do well in the new business environment that had been created by Reaganomics were those that had the capacity to be nimble by being lean and responsive to sharp sudden changes. One of the features of business growth that was common in the 1980s and 1990s was growth by acquisition (mergers). Peters did not believe that mergers and acquisitions were the answer to the problem most corporations faced. In fact, he was of the view that these were serving to compound their difficulties. He proposed that the businesses that would do well in the economic environment of the future would be smaller organizations with highly skilled workers.

Reimaginative leadership expressed in the modes of alternatives-thinking and staff empowerment requires an abundance mentality and a belief in the capacity of team members to make worthwhile contributions. There is the risk that some chaos may ensue, but this chaos can provide meaningful learning opportunities which if managed well can lead to the formation of a more confident and proficient team.

CHAPTER 4
Quality 3: Influence versus Power

Reimaginative leadership is appropriate for the twenty-first century as it relies more on influence than it does on power in decision-making and effecting organizational change and transformation. Influence is a greater source of motivation than power, as Zenger and Folkman (2013) and Damanpour (1991) have found.

The data from chapter two provide insights to support this claim. In table 2.2, the construct "uses influence rather than power to enforce will" is among the sub-factors of the variable "demonstrates care". A similar finding is made in table 2.3 where the same construct is found to be a sub-factor of the variable "creates conditions for staff members to participate in decision-making". The study conducted by the Gutfreund Intelligence Group, cited in chapter one, found that seventy-nine per cent of millennials surveyed want their boss to serve more as a coach or mentor. Mentors and coaches use influence rather than power to effect changes in the lives of mentees and coachees.

The concepts taken together suggest that there is an expectation on the part of employees that the leadership approach offered to them will be laden with influence and not dominated by power. If team members place great store in the principle of power-sharing, then effective leadership is more about influence than it is about power. The leader who relies on power to get people involved in the tasks to be pursued is a leader who faces the risk of diminishing returns. Such a leader also faces serious questions about the sustainability of the operations that are being undertaken. Leaders who are forced to rely on power are likely to be operating in competitive situations in which they are battling for ascendency and credibility or are struggling to stave off actual or perceived challenges to their authority.

Leaders who depend on power will have little efficacy in selling upwards and across, as power is only effective when one has control over those who must submit to one's power. Influential leaders, on the other hand, can produce desired results selling upwards, across and downwards. The influential leader seeks to persuade and relies on the credibility of their proposals and their potential value-added impact, not their power to force their will on others.

A principal in a school occupies a position of power but is at risk of undermining the credibility of that office, if they have to rely on the power of the office to get things done. The inherent strength and beauty of the office, and its capacity to produce desired results, depend on the degree to which the principal can inspire or positively influence others to play their role and give their best.

Definition of Influence

Influence may be defined as the capacity to produce a sustainable impact on the character and behaviour of a person (or a process), such that the character and consequently the behaviour reflects, at least in part, the vision, values, and desired outcomes of the person exercising the influence. Influence is the capacity to persuade, and to cause others to think and feel the ideas and emotions of the one seeking to exercise influence. Such capacity can cause movement (action) in the direction of the would-be influencer's wishes and objectives. Influence can be negative or positive. Negative influence occurs, for example, when an employee can convince a fellow employee to engage in behaviours such as stealing company property. Positive influence, on the other hand, occurs when a leader is able to stimulate and enlist the commitment of employees to a higher cause, whether the cause is the attainment of the goals of the organization, where the organization is involved in providing a service to the community, or some act of social responsibility where the organization is seeking to give back to the community. In this regard, positive influence is a species of *inspiration*. Power, on the other hand, is concerned with force of will and the power to make decisions and impose one's wishes on a person or process. While the use of power may produce desired behaviour changes, such changes are not likely to be sustained as the person has not been changed from within.

While "positive influence" and "inspiration" may be used interchangeably, they are not synonyms. Inspiration is a much higher form of engagement. An inspired individual or an inspiring moment is characterized by a near transcendental experience where the inner self connects to a powerful and persuasive presence that moves one to new heights of commitment and achievement that are extraordinary. Positive influence may thus be somewhat inspirational. But the focus on influence here is not so much to explain its relationship to inspiration but to create the distinction between the use of influence and power to get results. Power is based on force and the issuing of orders and commands. Influence is based on stimulation and the exposure to ideas and the invitation to participation. When one acts in response to power, fear rather than commitment is involved. When one acts based on positive influence, commitment and loyalty are triggered.

Therefore, influence may be described as positive when the action is undertaken without a sense of fear and a feeling on the part of the actor that the action is noble or necessary or the desirable thing to do. The extent to which one is willing to continue moving in the direction articulated by the influencer and can cause others (third party influence) to move in said direction, is the extent to which the influence has resulted in inspiration and is a measure of the effectiveness of the leader.

Leadership, Influence, and Relationships

Myatt (2012), in a passionate blog entitled "Leadership Influence and Relationships", argues that the reason some leaders have more influence than others, results from the decision some leaders make to invest more "in" others. He contends that those with influence have built into others, through some form of consistent direct or indirect contribution. Those with the greatest amount of influence

Quality 3: Influence versus Power

almost always have the strongest relationships. Myatt hypothesizes that if true leadership is about influence, then influence is about relationships, and relationships are about the investments made *into* people.

Myatt further opines that on close examination we find that the core characteristics of what really makes for great leadership is not power, title, authority, or even technical competency. He insists that what makes a leader truly great is the ability to both earn and keep the loyalty and trust of those whom they lead. Leadership, he insists, is about trust, stewardship, care, concern, service, humility and understanding. These qualities are created and sustained in relationships. By building trusting, accountable and caring relationships, we add to the lives of others, and in the process build a credit balance of goodwill, enabling us to draw heavily and win loyalty in good and bad times.

This kind of investment translates into bonds enabling a leader to succeed without reliance on positional authority as well as get past philosophical gaps, survive mistakes, challenges, downturns and other obstacles that will inevitably occur.

Myatt concludes that a leader does not change mindsets by being right, but by showing care. Noting that this conclusion should not be read as suggesting that logic and reason do not have their place, Myatt cautions that logic and reason rarely overcome strong emotional or philosophical positions. Trying to cram one's positional logic down the throat of others, will simply leave a very bad taste in their mouths. He offers a number of solutions for leaders struggling with their roles as a result of not being able to produce the results they desire.

Among the solutions Myatt suggests are:
- Clarifying the Vision
- Focusing on the positive
- Making others feel successful.

With a clear vision, there is a larger good and a defined goal towards which the influence is directed. By focusing on the positive, the energies of team members are not affected by cortisone and other hormones that result in the narrowing of blood vessels. By making others feel successful there is excitement and intellectual and emotional orgasmic thrill that predispose one to be expectant, cooperative, and willing.

Myatt's views are supported by findings in research that inform this work. Of the ninety-seven teachers who participated in the study, 96.9 either strongly agreed or agreed (70.1 per cent strongly agree and 26.8 per cent agree) that to be effective a principal should seek to influence rather than use power to enforce their will. The value placed on influence, and the framework within which they see it, are reflected in a strong correlation that the study found between the variables "seek to influence rather than use power to enforce will" and "advocate for justice"; a correlation of .570 was found.

The desire for involvement in decision-making and the perception that leaders are more effective when they use influence rather than power are not confined to teachers. This expectation exists among students as well as among workers in industries (Thompson 2009). This notion of workers' expectation of participation in decision-making is a settled issue, having been argued by a host of researchers particularly the human relations theorists and later contributors such as Manley (1975), Ouchi (1981) and Juran (2003). Thus, consultative leadership is expected not only in the contexts of schooling, but across the general workplace, as well as between leaders and the general citizenry.

The issue of participation arose as one of the four elements in the second round of analysis of the data, as discussed in chapter two. This finding reinforced the arguments not only of Manley, Ouchi, and Juran mentioned above but also of McClelland (1961) who made a compelling case of the worker's need for power as a fundamental requirement of a meaningful life. The fulfilment of that need for power is experienced through meaningful participation and involvement in the making of decisions which affect them. The global study by Gutfreund also reinforced this principle. Thus, in making the case for participation, Thompson (2017) in advancing Paradigm RePaDO, highlights an element of leadership which is at the forefront of leadership effectiveness. Leaders who do not actively seek to involve those they lead in the processes of decision-making and who do not define roles for each member of their teams while allowing those members to share in the shaping of those roles, risk isolation and demotivation of those workers as Thompson (2019b) argues in Proposition MRM.

Fullan (2007), in his compelling work *The New Meaning of Educational Change,* discusses the change process and poses a question concerning the propensity or willingness of human beings to change even when faced with the most contrastive of choices in even literal life or death options. Fullan notes that trying to scare people into a course of action does not often lead to compliance and threatening tough sanctions does not often lead to change in behaviour. The fact is, people will continue on a chosen lifestyle even when they are told that that lifestyle will lead to death. It takes more than scary tactics to change people; more than brute force; more than punishment. The easiest way to change behaviour is to invest in relationships and seek to influence the desired change. Fullan (2003) had somewhat laid the foundations for this argument upon which he elaborates in Fullan (2011), where he discusses the critical skills needed by the change leader, one of which is the capacity to persuade others to adopt new ways of working and serving, rather than seeking to force these new ways upon them.

Fullan's position is instructive, and appears to be supported by the opinions of the teachers in the 2013–2014 research. In the study, 81.4 per cent of respondents strongly agreed or agreed that an effective principal should resist dictating how staff members should think.

Generally, people – whether they be children or adults, whether in formal or informal settings, whether highly trained or novices – tend to recoil at being dictated to or at attempts to control them. Manipulating people into behaving in a particular manner can produce desired results but these outcomes are usually not sustainable and when people discover that they are being manipulated, trust is deeply (and in some cases, permanently) eroded.

Forms of Influence

The renowned author and motivational speaker Dick Biggs, in a 2005 blog, also makes the case that ultimately leadership is about influence and contends that there are seven (7) ways to influence people, noting that influence can be negative, neutral, or positive.

Dick Biggs (2005) lists three forms of negative influence techniques, namely, coercion, intimidation, and manipulation. Coercion can have the effect of producing short-term results but over time will result in a drop in employee morale and high turnover. Intimidation, he says, is the trademark of a dictator and works effectively with weak and insecure people, who will fall in line. But neither the weak and insecure employee, nor the confident and strong one will respect a leader who uses intimidation and what is certain is that both will resent such a leader. Manipulation is the craft of a one-sided win. A manipulative leader influences others to produce results that suit the leader's ego and desire to look impressive and some employees will become part of seemingly legitimate activities in support of the leader thinking that their interests are considered, only to discover later that they were being used. The result of leadership styles that manipulate is a distrustful and suspicious employee.

The leader who uses any of the above styles may feel at times that they good at what they do and that since leadership is about getting things done, any method is acceptable. Common sense suggests, however, that leadership by negative influencing brings only short-term wins. The respect lost and the resentment produced are never worth the short-term gains made, regardless of the degree to which the leader may think, or claim, that they do not care what others think or say about them.

Biggs also discusses neutral influence. This type of influence he calls *negotiation*. In bona fides negotiations, the aim of the leader is to find a solution that is fair to all concerned – the individuals and the organizations or groups. Such a solution will be a win-win one rather than a win-lose (where the leader wins and the others lose) or lose-win (where the leader loses, and others win). Win-win solutions do not mean that everyone gets what they want. Rather, win-win means that each feels the outcome is reasonable and that even where sacrifices were made, what one had to give up was not disproportionate to what others had to give up or what one was hoping to get.

Negotiation is predicated on the view that the right answer is not obvious and that the best outcome may be a compromise. Obviously, not all situations in which a leader must decide can be subject to negotiation. The sage leader will know when negotiation is the most appropriate way in which to search for a solution. By virtue of being *neutral,* this style of influence is helpful when the leader is open to a range of possible outcomes.

Rounding out his list of seven influence techniques, Biggs lists persuasion, education, and inspiration as the three forms of positive influence. The energy required to persuade will depend on how skeptical the listener is and how much information they may require to be moved. The key to effective persuasion, in my view, is found in showing how the proposed course of action is in one's best interest. Closely allied to persuasion is education, which is made effective through using hard facts and logic. However hard the facts may be, there may still be skepticism unless the leader is able to communicate these facts in a manner that touches the emotions and gives the inspirational sense that the proposed course of action is simply the right thing to do.

Summary

The insights in this chapter suggest that one effective way to motivate employees to support the decisions and strategies of the organization is to use persuasion and influence rather than the force of executive power. This is not to suggest that reimaginative leadership is averse to the use of power, rather the suggestion is that the leader who is reimagining how to motivate others will rely less on power and more on influence. The data from the study of millennials also support the notion that collegial and egalitarian approaches to the exercise of power, and the reliance on negotiation and persuasion are the ways in which people in the twenty-first century prefer to be led.

It is acknowledged that influence can be both positive and negative and each has different nuances. This means that a leader who is committed to directing and leading through influence rather than through instruction and commands will need to expose themselves to the various nuances of influence in taking account of the facts of each situation in which a decision is to be made.

CHAPTER 5
Quality 4: Mutual Accountability

Reimaginative leadership is predicated upon values such as egalitarianism, power-sharing, inclusive decision-making processes, and transparency. Mutual accountability may be described as a leadership doctrine which stipulates that persons in positions of power who seek to hold others accountable, must themselves be willing to submit to be held accountable by those they lead. Indeed, the moral authority to hold others accountable is grounded in the willingness to submit oneself to be held accountable.

The data in chapter two highlight the underlying principles of mutual accountability at several levels. In the first place the subfactor "responds differently when there is disagreement", located in table 2.2 under the factor "demonstrates care", suggests that employees expect that leaders will show regard for their points of view and will treat differing points of view as a positive thing. Inherent in this is the notion that the leader is prepared to allow competing ideas to have a reasonable chance of being considered when decisions are to be made. This is one level at which a leader shows accountability to others. This notion is further supported by the subfactor "willing to debate issues in situations where opinions differ" which is found under the factor "utilize the diverse strengths of members of staff" found at the top of the third column in table 2.3. A leader's posture of being willing to debate points of view and to place themselves in the same space with those they lead is a powerful statement of showing that they consider self as answerable to those they lead.

The picture of mutual accountability becomes even more compelling when the subfactor "admits error when established" found under factor "shows willingness to accept criticism" is considered. It is a confident leader who respects the independence of the thoughts of others and who does not see themselves as a god who is unwilling to admit error their junior team members.

The kinds of behaviours described above are not easy. They require deep self-confidence and personal strength. Indeed, the commitment to mutual accountability is the touchstone of reimaginative leadership.

Mills-Schofield (2012) argues that accountability means putting our word and reputation on the line resulting in others counting on us to deliver in keeping with our promise. A publicly expressed or privately written statement about what one will or will not do is the starting point of the act of being accountable. Members of a professional body, which is governed by a code of ethics, automatically commit to be accountable to the principles of the code and to be held responsible if they fail so to do.

Bivins (2006) begins at an even more basic starting point and cites the Australian ethicist Will Barret who contends that accountability is inherently an issue of morality and ultimately it is one's word and oneself that have been placed in the public square for testing. Lehmann's (2006) suggestion about the starting point of ethics is a compelling argument in support of the view that accountability is a moral issue. Lehmann contends that in determining the correct course of action that one may take, the primary question should not be "what ought I to do?", but "who am I?". By beginning with the question of who one is, then the issue of moral responsibility moves from being something imposed externally to one imposed internally.

Accountability is firstly a matter of personal morality and is based on a determination of who one is and who one seeks to be. Thus, accountability is not so much about what others expect of us but the standards to which we are willing to hold ourselves. It is this question of the standard to which we are willing to hold ourselves that introduces the question of mutual responsibility.

Defining Mutual Accountability

The term *mutual accountability* is used most frequently in the field of development co-operation and generally refers to a process by which two (or multiple) partners agree to be held responsible for commitments voluntarily made to each other. The Organization for Economic Cooperation and Development (OECD) posits that mutual accountability relies on trust and partnership around shared agendas rather than on hard sanctions and on encouraging the behaviour change needed to meet commitments.

The issue of mutual accountability was a centrepiece of the Paris Declaration on Climate Change, and in elaborating on the meaning of mutual accountability, the interpretation of the concept as outlined in the Accra Agenda for Action was referenced. The Accra Agenda contends that accountability plays a key role in shaping the quality of governance at national, local, and international levels, which involves transparency of conduct as developing and donor countries collaborate to pursue development results including the reduction of poverty.

The understanding of mutual accountability as used in the literature on development cooperation is helpful in defining mutual accountability as a construct in reimaginative leadership. The two key principles are (a) the purpose of ends for which mutual accountability is sought, and (b) the process by which it is achieved. In development cooperation the purpose may be broadly described as that of reducing inequity and inequality which will become measured in the reduction of poverty and the process is one of transparently insisting that each side keeps the promises it makes.

Leadership is an act by which an organization is enabled to successfully achieve the goals it sets itself. Accountability is critical to the execution of leadership as leaders are expected to make commitments to the organization and on behalf of the organization concerning the things the organization will deliver. The making of such commitments and the assessment of the extent to which they are kept must be open for all interested parties to know and examine.

An excellent self-governing maxim is, "under-promise and over-deliver". In performance management discussions with team members, I stress the importance of keeping promises. In closing many leadership training sessions, the summary of the main take-away points invariably includes, "keep your promises". In my mind it is simply the leader-like and honourable thing to do. Everyone will, at one time or another, break a solemn promise. Given this reality, the discussion about making and keeping promises should not be about whether others have broken promises but the extent to which each giver of promises keeps them, that is, how many are kept. If a political or organizational leader or any employee in an organization repeatedly fails to keep promises they make, then there must be an issue of credibility, competence, and/or experience.

The underlying meaning of a promise is that the maker is submitting themselves to others with the request that by making pledges they are asking to be held accountable for delivering on the pledges made. Although this is what a promise means, some leaders get upset when they are asked about their promises if the date for delivery has passed. In Jamaica it can be a dangerous thing to comment on whether political leaders have kept their promises. But leaders who have high regard for those they lead, and employees who are highly professional, take pride in having their performance assessed relative to the promises they make.

Mutual Accountability Begins with Personal Accountability

Mutual accountability begins with personal accountability and personal accountability is the quintessential criterion for organizational, community and national success. On this basis, everyone who has attained the capacity to reason simultaneously assumes some degree of leadership accountability. Personal accountability is critical to the success of every successful organization.

Personal accountability may be seen, for example, in the self-critical and solutions-oriented engagement of a team member who, despite being located at a junior level in an organization's hierarchy, assumes the responsibility for ensuring that they offer constructive suggestions for how the organization may improve itself. The team member who understands that personal accountability is an ingredient in personal as well as organizational success is unlikely to be a "yes" person who simply does what they are told regardless of whether or not there may be errors in the communication or a lack of awareness, on the part of the person giving the directions, of relevant facts that are in their (that is, the recipient's) possession.

The team member who demonstrates leadership by showing personal accountability is willing to interrogate the views and proposed paths and programmes of the organization. They are also prepared to offer their own ideas and suggestions on how the goals and objectives may be attained using what may be the more effective approaches. In organizational cultures in which individuals assume personal responsibility the practice of "yesmanship" is unlikely to flourish. "Yesmanship" which involves blindly following the dictates of a leader and refusing or being unwilling to hold them accountable is one of the manifestations of lack of mutual accountability.

The adage "the boss is always right" is just that – an adage. This notion came out of the "scientific" era of the early twentieth century and has its genesis in the doctrine of Frederick Taylor and Henri Fayol who (along with others) advanced the view that there was "one best way" to get the job done and workers needed to be trained in specific ways to be able to carry out the tasks of the organization. While no reasonable person would dispute the importance of training, it is self-evidently senseless to construct the training of human beings in ways similar to that of training dogs and horses. In *training* animals, the important element is the ability to follow instruction and to execute according to prescribed ways. The element of *thinking* is what is missing. Thus, the average worker during the 1900–1930s (the scientific era) was expected to be good at remembering and to executing consistent with instructions.

This kind of approach to using human resources works well when the tasks are repetitive and straightforward and the context predictable. In contexts of uncertainty even when the tasks are routine such as in customer service, workers must be able to troubleshoot and innovate or at least think outside the box. To simply do as one is told can prove unhelpful or even harmful to the organization.

The higher in the organizational hierarchy an employee is, the greater the need for critical thinking which, for all intents and purposes, is the antithesis of "yesmanship". A leader who is surrounded by "yes" men and women, could take the organization down a cliff. It is unfortunate when an organization finds itself in a situation in which its senior managers do not have the courage to say to the team leader, "but sir" or "boss, that cannot work". Over my twenty plus years of working with several organizations I have sat in many managers' meetings and tried to nudge my colleagues to exercise the basic act of responsible followership of simply asking "why?". Many senior managers sit and listen to the leader articulate (sometimes opaquely) a new direction and yet give their assent by deafening silence, sometimes broken only by a weak murmur. Sometimes the result of that form of engagement (or disengagement) can be costly to the organization.

Leadership's Responsibility to Actively Engage Stakeholders

Sometimes the disengagement of team members is a function of both fear and frustration. Some senior and middle managers who withdraw from engagement with the processes of decision-making do so because they have seen what happens to their colleagues who speak up or have simply decided that the pain and stress associated with having their views heard is not worth the effort. Many report that in the end, even though their views may be given some form of "hearing", the course of direction is not changed, and another set of ill-fated strategies are implemented. In many cases it is those same managers who had become tired of trying to say "no, there is a better way", who are called upon to pick up the pieces after another failed programme or project.

Kelley (1992) provides a perspective on followership. While agreeing with the general descriptions offered by Kelley, I prefer to refer use the word "leaders" where he uses "followers". Kelley's categories are as follows:

- **Alienated followers (leaders)** are mavericks who have a healthy scepticism of the organization. They are capable, but cynical.
- **Conformist followers (leaders)** are the "yes people" of the organizations. They are very active at doing the organization's work and will actively obey orders.
- **Passive followers (leaders)** rely on leaders to do the thinking for them. They also require constant direction.
- **Exemplary followers (leaders)** are independent, innovative, and willing to question leadership. This type of employee is critical to organizational success. Exemplary employees know how to work well with others.

Organizations that succeed in contexts of uncertainty, complexity and chaos will require the presence of what Kelley calls, exemplary followers and what I describe as conscientious leadership. Conscientious leaders are those who approach their work with a critical-thinking perspective and who are mindful that their task is not simply to do as they are told but to use their creativity to get the job done well.

Many organizations set out to recruit the type of employees who possess the qualities of *conscientious* leaders but because of outmoded styles of leadership produce *alienated* leaders in the short to medium term. Hersey and Blanchard (1982), in their situational leadership theory, argued that successful leadership is achieved by selecting a style based on follower readiness. Their basic argument is that the style adopted by the leader should be informed by the point (of consciousness) at which the follower is.

The word "follower" is not an appropriate designation and suggests that every employee should be seen as a leader having a different level of responsibility. Thus, while I agree with Hersey and Blanchard that different situations may call for a different approach to leadership, the key determinant should not be characterized as "follower-readiness" but *levels of accountability* and *critical-thinking engagement*. If employees are consistently treated as followers, then a certain type of behaviour will become normative. If, on the other hand, they are treated as leaders then a different type of behaviour will become the norm. Consequently, leaders by their approach to leadership can produce uncritical "yes-ers" who will repeat in their work any error that was inherent in the instruction, or they will produce critical thinkers who ask "why" and who are willing to innovate and thus stand a better chance of improving the quality of output.

It is perhaps the case that some leadership personalities tend to naturally produce different forms of personal accountability covering the range of tendencies outlined by Kelley. While the leader may, as an act of common sense, adopt a style that is informed by the readiness of team members, there is a responsibility that each leader has to ensure that they retain the capacity to be critical, innovative and productive.

Barbara Kellerman of the John F. Kennedy school of government at Harvard University, in her pioneering 2008 work, *Followership: How Followers are Creating Change*, argues that the needs of followers are every bit as important as the needs of leaders. Kellerman's point can be extended to posit that the needs of all members of the team should be treated with importance, even if all needs cannot be addressed at the same time – as will likely be the case. But one common need that all team members have is that of a working environment in which they feel valued and where they are given an opportunity to bring their knowledge and skills to influence the direction of the organization.

The necessity of creating a working environment in which team members can be exemplary is because we no longer live in an era of restricted access to knowledge and followers have access to information that can inform the creation of useful ideas to advance the organization. No single person can keep abreast with all the relevant new knowledge being created. The smart and effective leader will, therefore, be the one who has learned how to engage the multiple ideas and diverse perspectives in finding solutions to the complex problems of the modern workplace.

The Non-Negotiable Obligation to Remain Personally Accountable

It is not enough, however, for team members to blame team leaders for alienating them and in the process to disassociate themselves from the unacceptable outcomes of the organization. Team members who take the business of personal accountability seriously and who are committed to adding value to the organization have an appreciation for the fact that team leaders are not likely, nor should be expected, to be "yes" men and women any more than team members should not. Team members should expect that they may face resistance and opposition to their ideas from team leaders in the same way that they sometimes resist and oppose the ideas of team leaders. This inevitable (and desirable) tension and sometimes clash of ideas (and sometimes personalities) form the milieu for the organization's progress and requires on team members' part the qualities of *self-transcendence, perseverance, and advocacy skills.*

Self-transcendence, as argued earlier, is the commitment not to be limited by one's personal interests or one's perspectives on issues. One of the important expressions of that commitment is the placement of priorities related to self, compared to the priorities related to the organization. The placement of these priorities reflects the degree to which one is transcending self. The opposite of self-transcendence is self-entrapment. Self-entrapment involves myopic pre-occupation with self – how much attention one gets in terms of status, perks, prominence, position, pay, power, and privileges.

Summary

Mutual accountability is predicated on the philosophy that those who lead have a duty to hold themselves accountable to those they lead and to be willing to be held accountable. The idea of being accountable affirms an acknowledgement that others can provide meaningful insights which can assist the leader improve, thus the need for willingness to accept correction and openness to criticism. Mutual accountability has been described as the touchstone of reimaginative leadership because the act of a leader being willing to submit themselves to subordinates and to be guided by their counsel and to learn from their criticisms takes a great deal of personal courage and maturity.

When the leader of an organization subscribes to the principle of mutual accountability, they contribute to the creation of a culture in which responsible conduct is more easily cultivated as other members of the organization will likely be led to reckon that they too must be willing to take account of the criticisms of peers and subordinates and learn from them. The likely result is that members of the organization will be more thoughtful and diligent in the execution of their duties and responsibilities, mindful that their peers and subordinates will be looking on at any moment.

The attainment of a culture of mutual accountability in an organization is not easy and given the level of mistrust which pervades organizations (Hurley 2006), team members, even those in senior positions are prone to "keep their mouths shut". Thus, the process of creating a culture of mutual accountability requires organizational policies, backed-up by guarantees that there can be no retribution for asking tough questions, and offering criticisms, of superiors. There will also need to be reward systems which reinforce behaviours which are consistent with the principles of mutual accountability.

CHAPTER 6
Qualities 5 and 6: Change Catalysation and Courage

The capacity to manage and the willingness to embrace change are among the top skills required of leaders in the twenty-first century. These behaviours will invariably require courage. The *Cambridge Dictionary* (2019) defines courage as the ability to do something dangerous, or to face pain or opposition.

The act of continuously reimagining inescapably means that there is the likelihood that the way things are at a given time will not be the way they are after an engagement in reimagination. Moving from the status quo to a reimagined new place involves change and will likely incur opposition. The act of pursuing that reimagined new future in the face of opposition calls for courage.

The organization which invests in, and encourages critical thinking, opens up to the prospects of change, undertakes change and responds to changing situations. Some of the changes which an organization must undertake will often require courage on the part of its leaders.

It has been noted (Thompson 2019a) that confronting and effecting change is one of the most present and potent realities which face organizations. According to Scandura and Sharif (2011) technological changes, process-oriented changes and people-oriented changes are all part of the tapestry of life in organizations. Organizations must be constantly changing in order to survive the turbulent and changing realities of the contexts within which they operate. One important task of leaders then is how to manage change. Kotter (1996) develops an eight-step change model in which creating a sense of urgency about the need for change is the first step. To the extent that Kotter is correct, then it means that one critical skill of a leader in the twenty-first century is the ability to successfully articulate the case for change.

Organizational change is related to chaos theory and organizational development theory and more specifically the notion of dynamical instability. The concept of dynamical instability was first advanced by the physicist Henri Poincare who contends that even apparent lack of order in a system obeys laws or rules. The two main components of chaos theory are the ideas that even the most complex systems rely upon an underlying order, and that very simple or small systems and events can cause very complex behaviours or events.

Reimaginative leadership is connected to, and informed by, this conception of chaos theory in two respects. Firstly, it is an approach to leadership that, by virtue of its questioning of the current situation (the status quo), injects transformative instability into the organization by questioning, wondering, and proposing. Miller and Rollnick (2012) suggest that this approach is useful for the functioning of educational institutions, arguing that given global and regional factors such as globalization, migration, performativity pressures, educational institutions must undertake changes.

Reimaginative leadership then, as a mode of behaviour, disturbs the status quo and is informed by an underlying belief that new ways of behaving and relating and higher levels of excellence can come out of the chaotic contexts of ruffled feathers and bruised egos. Thus, the leader who is engaged in reimaginative thinking, while not being naïve to issues of protocol and politics in the organization, will not be held hostage to expectations, pressures, or fears but will pursue an agenda of radical change even though the endpoint of that radical change may be preceded by some confusion, uncertainty, hostility and seeming failure. The modus operandi of reimaginative leadership is not that what exists is useless or defective but that whatever the state of what exists, however good, it can be made better. Thus, in the thinking and practice of reimaginative leadership there is a default setting that communicates that even previously *imaginative* ideas need to be revisited and critiqued in order that the organization may create solutions that are appropriate for its current and future contexts.

Reimaginative leadership is a mode of leading which moves the individual and the organization to reject one-dimensional reiterations of what is, or a discussion on what *cannot be*, and instead engages in in-depth reflection on approaches and possibilities that are venturesome, risk-taking, and informed. Through these articulations, the leader shapes new visions of the possible and seeks to recruit commitment to the cause of pursuing uncharted waters towards a transformed organization and society. Reimagination is the gift that empowers us to resist being conscripted into the despairing conformity of the notion that suggests that 'nothing can be done and nothing will change'. Reimagination is the counter-intuitive consciousness that alerts us to the fact that by buying into the notion that we can do nothing to change the way things are, we risk becoming nothing ourselves and the legacy we leave is nothingness.

Subversive and Constructive Change

Reimaginative leadership involves a critical reflection on, and appraisal of, one's status quo with a view to enhancing it and raising it to a higher level. The reimaginative leader is never automatically satisfied with things as they are, simply because things are working (for example the organization is profitable, and people appear comfortable). Rather, the reimaginative leader operates with a nimbleness of notion and perspective that assumes that regardless of how well an organization is doing there will always be room for higher levels of excellence.

The process of nurturing new thinking and disturbing old systems of thought in others and organizations often requires, perhaps often, the skills of constructive subversion. Subversion suggests the replacement of ideology or way of life (which is itself informed by some ideology) and the insertion or installation of a new way of doing thinking and doing business. Constructive subversion suggests a commitment to a greater good. It is not simply an agenda for change, it is an agenda for delivering value. To be sure, perspectives of what actions have the potential to deliver value are subjective; but a person who is pursuing an agenda of constructive subversion decides as to what the endgame looks like (what, or the objective) after resolving two important "hows". The "what" refers to the value that the subversion seeks to deliver and the "how" refers to; (a) the path to be taken, and (b) the partners to be engaged. Constructive subversion then, is not subversion for its own sake, it is subversion that is purpose-driven, path-defined and partner-welcoming (even though many constructive subversive activities may suffer from the lack of partners in the early stages of the effort).

Jan Kippers Black in a seminal 2009 work entitled, *The Politics of Human Rights Protection*, catalogues aspects of human history in seeking to show how often leaders and followers had failed to be as responsible and thorough as they might have been and the consequences of that failure. Black introduces the idea of *constructive subversion* and begins the chapter by referencing a speech given in 1973 by US Senator Hubert Humphrey in which Humphrey commented on the Watergate scandal. The essence of Humphrey's remarks, and the point that Black seeks to illustrate, is that a salient feature of Watergate was that there were persons who knew what the right thing was to do but failed to insist that the right thing be done. The story of Watergate was about how power corrupts and the dangers that can befall an organization when followers (aides, advisors, employees) allow themselves to become easily conscripted into, and loyal supporters of, questionable causes in situations in which they have a duty to say "no" and to use their influence and resolve to overturn (subvert) causes and projects that are harmful to the body politic.

The underlying argument of both Black and Humphrey is that there are situations in which the official agenda and mission deserve to be subverted and overthrown if it can be shown, or if there is good cause to believe, that that agenda and mission are inconsistent with the ideals and core values of the organization and if unavoidable harm is likely to be done. The required acts of subversion may come from any level of leadership in the organization.

Kotter (2013) expresses exasperation at notions that a few extraordinary people at the top can provide all the leadership needed in an organization and he suggests that to expect that this will be so is not only ridiculous, but a recipe for failure. Kotter insists that in an ever-faster-moving world, leadership is increasingly needed from more and more people, no matter where they are in a hierarchy.

Features of Constructive Subversion

The notion of subversion, as a modality of leadership, may carry undertones of aggression, stridency, and even impoliteness, even when expressed in the context of the contest of ideas and approaches. Such undertones are not intended. What the idea seeks to convey is a commitment on the part of leadership to the diligent pursuit of alternatives, mindful of how the status quo seeks to protect and defend the practices with which it has become comfortable. Constructive subversion then is intended to highlight the fact that very often, an organization's pursuit of excellence requires radical change in order for that change to be realized. It may be helpful, in this regard, to consider that the Latin root of the word 'radical' is *radix* which means root. Thus, the idea of radical or subversive change means getting to the root of the influence of the undesired situation and effecting the change.

Based on the foregoing, constructive subversion may be deemed to have three components. First, it is *disruptive*. In undertaking its *disruptive* agenda, constructive subversion causes change and stimulates dialogue towards renewal. The persistent engagement in that dialogue or the persistence with which the disrupter places ideas into the space for conversation will force others to contend with the challenge and call towards renewal. In other words, the disruptive agenda of the constructive subversionist is not simply about stimulating a conversation or debate, rather it is about forging paths towards action. The disruptive character of reimaginative leadership is informed by the consciousness that what is, the status quo, is not inevitable and not necessarily the most optimum way of being, behaving, and operating and that there are better ways of doing things.

The second component of constructive subversion is that it is *dialogical*. The constructive subversionist engages in dialogue both with those who are the guardians of the status quo and those who, though not guardians, may be opposed to the path of disruption that is being pursued. The purpose of this dialogue is three-fold as outlined in figure 6.1.

Figure 6.1: Three-Fold Purpose of Constructive Subversion Dialogue

1. To convince the guardians of the status quo that there is a better way and to, hopefully win some level of support, but if not to create a degree of discomfort and consciousness.

2. To gain insights to refine and sharpen the disruptive, constructivist agenda. By hearing what others believe, by understanding what they oppose in the subversion agenda, the disruptor can sharpen the message and win greater support.

3. Self-critique. A re-imaginative leader, as I have argued, is never satisfied that what is, is the best. By the same token, regardless of how convinced a constructive subversionist is about the merits of a cause and the appropriateness of the methods being employed, he or she remains open to pushing self to find better ways of pursuing that agenda.

The third component or element of constructive subversion is *determination*. Organizations and the defenders of the status quo are not likely to concede ground willingly and give in, in the face of questions about their mode of operation. There will be fierce opposition and push back which can become nasty and personal. One has only to recall the punishing and nasty pushback that Martin Luther King faced as he challenged segregation and abuse of human rights in America. He and many of his supporters were imprisoned on spurious charges or otherwise denied their civil liberties. Even members of the faith community pushed back against him. King (1963) in his famous letter from prison sent to bishops of eight faith communities, defended his efforts and method of seeking a more just and equitable society. King contended that the scale of injustice was such that the efforts at social change could not wait, as some members of the church community were suggesting.

Nelson Mandela's attempt to end apartheid in South Africa ranks as another constructively subversive undertaking embedded, as was the case with King, in amazing courage and determination. Mandela's act of courage did not, however, come from a place of fearlessness. Mandela (1994) shares that he had days of fear and anxiety. These fears and anxieties led him to define courage not as fearlessness but the willingness to do the thing one feels called upon to do, or doing the risky even when feeling fearful, as he explains.

Constructive subversion often appears from below but may also come from the top. As a movement from below, constructive subversion may occur when a low-level employee sees the need for change and works for change. As an initiative from the top, constructive subversion occurs when a CEO (or a principal, a parson, a police chief) sees the need to replace a culture of lack of accountability, indifference to excellence and sloppy service with one that is built on accountability, excellence, and superior service. The conditions of lack of accountability, indifference to excellence and sloppy service sometimes become the norm in an organization and where the leadership seeks to revamp and renew, the leadership may be faced with resistance, not only from within but without. Many CEOs sometimes lose their jobs trying to constructively subvert old systems that are proving counterproductive to the common good. Others survive and succeed. Replacing a corrosive and obstructive culture with one that is customer-centred, service-driven and committed to excellence is not always easy and requires courage, determination, persistence, high advocacy skills and clarity of conviction.

In many cases however, the need to engage in subversive activity is warranted. Constructive subversion is a response to the subtle forms of self-satisfaction with existing levels of success and the indifference that can arise in a context of limited business competition. In those instances, the subversion requires a higher form of advocacy and nuanced perspicacity that enables the reimaginative leader to articulate the need for nimbleness and rigour in the prevailing circumstances and fashion a future that is inviting, challenging and motivating. This form of reimagination need not be seen as the purview of those in official leadership positions. Rather, it can be undertaken by anyone courageous enough to dare to question the current order and diligent enough to describe the possible future, though doing so involves great risk of which those undertaking these efforts must be aware.

Constructive subversion then, is both the potent antidote for, and the tenacious gadfly of, indolence, smug self-satisfaction, indifference, myopia, dis-rigour, feeble-mindedness, entropy, and unison with the status quo. If one wishes to undertake a constructive subversive journey, one must be prepared to go it alone, as well as being cautious of the motives of those who seek to join as some may do so, not based on a belief in a larger cause, but based on an opportunistic intent. The pursuit of a constructive subversion journey also requires that one be very clear on one's objective for there will be those whose criticism will be designed to question the purity and value of the objective in ways that can cause the subversionist to doubt themselves and withdraw from the pursuit. Constructive subversion requires tenacity.

Reimaginative Leadership as Courage

Leadership which seeks to reimagine a new future (as did Martin Luther King and Nelson Mandela, as well as others who have led protest movements such as "Occupy Wall Street" in the United States, and "#Feesmustfall" in the United Kingdom) requires courage. The Cambridge English dictionary offers a compelling definition of courage. That source suggests that courage may be defined as the ability to control one's fear in dangerous or difficult situations and to be willing to pursue the objectives in which one believes despite the risks to which one may be exposed.

In an organization in which dissent or critical thinking is not encouraged, it requires courage to criticize, or offer alternatives to, the dominant culture of the organization. There are anecdotal stories of organizations undertaking re-structuring exercises primarily for the purposes of getting rid of dissenters, even though the justification offered for such exercises is invariably quite different. In the data discussed in chapter two, we note from table 2.2 that the second variable which accounted for the variation in the data is "takes interest in the opinions of staff" and as can be seen in figure 2.1, that variable accounted for over twenty per cent of the variation in the data. Taking time to listen and considering the opinions of staff are acts of leadership which staff members will always welcome (Thompson 2018c).

Courage as Constructive Engagement with Others

Leadership assumes followership and thus one of the basic marks of an effective leader will be the extent to which they are able to attract and retain followers. One of the potential pitfalls of leadership, however, is that of a leader becoming consumed with self to the point of undertaking leadership in a manner wherein followers are treated as tools and accessories for the pursuit of ego-satisfaction and self-glory. While it is not the fault of a leader if members of the organization allow themselves to be used as mere props in their personal script of seeking greatness, it highlights the need for a level of consciousness on the part of the leader to be mindful of how they relate to others.

One of the insights gleaned from the data in chapter two is that staff expect to be given opportunities to develop themselves and responsiveness to this need is seen as an act of justice. Another insight that is of relevance to this question of the engagement between the leader and those they lead is the issue of using the diverse strengths of staff and promoting a culture of collective responsibility. The issue of using the diverse strengths of staff is one of the top three factors which accounted for the variation in the data in the second round of analysis as shown in table 2.3. "Promoting collective responsibility" is one of the subfactors. Both acts require some measure of courage in the sense that by nurturing and encouraging the expression of the talents of members of the organization, the leader risks the competition of others' performance getting attention and possibly recognition. For some leaders this competition can be perceived as threatening.

The creation of a culture in which collective responsibility is normative means that the leader will be treating their staff not merely as followers but as partners. Such an approach will require that the leader sees themselves as an ally or mentor. This approach is found to resonate with millennials, currently the dominant demographic of the twenty-first century.

The view that reimaginative leadership involves and requires constructive engagement with others (followers as partners and team members) is predicated, on the one hand, on the common sense principle that wisdom does not reside only with those who lead. In this regard it is instructive that the data on which this study relies, found that employees expect that the leader will trust in the collective wisdom of staff as shown in table 2.3. This act of trusting in the collective wisdom of staff is one of six leadership behaviours which Thompson (2018c) found to be trust-producing behaviours of leaders. A leader's effectiveness and an organization's success in innovation will depend on the degree to which they can inspire trust (Bartsch, Ebers and Maurer 2013; Gibbons 2004).

Another reason constructive engagement between leaders and those led calls for some measure of courage is grounded in the fact that the twenty-first century is the era of the commoditization of knowledge. This fact means, among other things, that much of what a leader knows about developments in an industry such as new practice models, changes in customer behaviour or expectations, new technologies, and so on, members of the team may also know. There is even the probability that some members of the organization may have more content knowledge and expertise than the leader does. Rather than being a threat to the leadership and the stability of the organization this reality should be a strength; but in the real world of human egos, this is not always the case and sometimes the expertise of members of the team may be seen as a threat by the leader. Using the definition that courage means proceeding to do what needs to be done despite feeling a sense of fear or sensing danger, it may be argued that it is okay for the leader to feel some amount of discomfort or apprehension, but their reimaginative commitment and capabilities will serve to lead them to engage, to debate, to doubt, to acknowledge being in the dark, in the face of the superior knowledge of a subordinate.

The foregoing assertions are partly grounded in the data discussed in chapter two. Table 2.3 shows that one of the subfactors which gives meaning to the variable "create conditions for staff members to participate in decision-making" is "regard for professional judgement of staff members". This subfactor suggests that members of a team expect that the leader will show regard for their professional judgement and expertise. Alongside this expectation that leaders will trust the professional judgement and expertise of team members is the expectation that the leader would defer to others who may be more knowledgeable on issues, than them. This expectation is listed as one of the subfactors of embracing the diverse strengths of staff as shown in the third column of table 2.3.

This foregoing analysis suggests that the leader has a duty to engage even when they feel somewhat insecure, or uncomfortable or even threatened. The act of engaging team members within the context of seeking to benefit from their professional judgement has the added dimension of making ideas, rather than individuals, superior. This further implies that authority lies not so much with an office or its holder, which is the traditional interpretation of power and authority, but with an idea. When that idea is tested and enriched by the collective wisdom it is likely to be superior in quality than an idea or decision coming from the leader which has not been tested or in relation to which there has been no debate.

Thus, the act of engagement and the opening of space for expert input and the use of the method of debate to test ideas amount to what may be called submission to a higher authority, namely the authority of the collective wisdom produced from the crucible of deep, collective reflection and debate. On the question of the role of debate in leadership and decision-making, the data in chapter two suggest that staff members expect that leaders will be willing to engage in debate where opinions differ.

The assertion that engaging staff in debate is a quality of reimaginative leadership, does not amount to a contention that all decisions must be subject to this process. Rather, what is being advanced is the idea that a culture of consultation and reliance on the wisdom of team members and the submission of the leadership to the higher authority of ideas rather than individuals provides the organization with more advantages in the making of complex decisions. The late Scott Peck in his moving classic, *A World Waiting to be Born: Civility Re-Discovered*, suggests that the most ungodly person is one who recognizes and respects no other authority or point of view, than their own. The capacity to submit to others, whose collective wisdom is deemed superior to one's own wisdom, is perhaps one of the most inclusive acts of leadership.

This approach to leading is informed by an assumption that the ideas and interpretations of *any* team member may have merit. Allocating time for each idea to be heard is potentially time-consuming and chaotic. But as Janis (1982a) found in his discussion on "groupthink", organizations which allow for a wider range of perspectives in decision-making do consume more time but invariably end up with better decisions.

It is to be recognized, however, that the process of producing a so-called collective position can be flawed. Lobbying behind the scenes does take place. Vested interests in one outcome, as against another, can influence how people read facts. The corrupting influence of special favour and even herd mentality in contexts where there is dis-familiarity with heterogeneity can all serve to undermine the attainment of a truly rigorous search for the most effective and efficient way forward. In the end it boils down to the integrity of the leader and their commitment to facilitating a truly multi-minded approach to solving an organizational problem.

The leader who possesses the capacity to submit to the multi-minded and collective wisdom of others, may become impatient about the pace of implementation, and one recognizes that there are simply some calls that the leader must make on the spur of the moment and in relation to which broad-based consultation is impossible. But the focus of the principle is not on emergencies, though it does invite consideration as to what is defined as emergencies. The focus of the principle of engagement is on how the leader approaches consultation, if at all they consult.

The character of unimaginative leadership versus reimaginative leadership may be seen in the difference between a manager who tells their officers what they want done, how they want it done and when they want it done as compared to another who, while having a very clear sense of what they want done and how it might be done, is seized of the fact that team members invest more in an initiative when they have a hand in shaping it. Thus, instead of telling their troops what they want and how they wish to have it done, the reimaginative leader shares the desired outcome and asks them how they think it can accomplished. Invariably, team members will collectively conceive of an approach that is either as effective as what the manager had in mind, or better. The fact that the suggested approach of the team members may be a copy of what the manager had in mind does not mean that value has not been derived from the consultation. Indeed, tremendous value, in the form of collective ownership and the motivation that comes from the feeling of being respected for the ideas one can contribute, is released into the initiative by that act of consultation. In addition, trust has been earned, capacity has been built or reinforced, and confidence for future endeavours has been procured.

Courage as Perseverance

Another important word in the lexicon of reimaginative leadership is *perseverance*. Perseverance is closely aligned to courage. The courageous leader, whose reimaginative vision of the future leads them to question the status quo and propose solutions for improving the state of affairs, will face repeated obstacles, some of which are subtle and sinister. The issue of perseverance is to be understood in the context of a leader seeking to bring an alternative vision to bear on the organization. For this agenda to be credible, the leader must be able to state very clearly and very simply what the end game is. The leader must be able to say what changes are being sought, why they are being sought, and how the changed situation will impact the lives of others living in the status quo. This is what clarity of purpose is all about. When the purpose is not clear it is almost inevitable that the descriptions of the agenda will suffer from multiple variations and in the end leave others confused and uncertain as to what is the real objective. The objective that a leader is pursuing should be capable of being reduced to a clear, simple and concise message. If not, the objective is likely to be viewed as suspect and most certainly will suffer negative morphs in transmission.

The leader who is pursuing an agenda of renewal must possess, if they are to be successful in winning support, a healthy appetite for opposing views. This healthy appetite is necessary in order to enable the leader to be open to other useful ideas from others. The ideas of opponents can serve the useful purpose of providing talking points which enrich and clarify the core message as well as provide the platform for answering concerns and questions that others have raised. If the leader is hostile to opposing views it becomes difficult for them to incorporate those views into the message being sold.

The second reason comfort with opposition helps with perseverance is that people have more patience for our ideas when we show respect and patience for theirs. The reimaginative leader does not live under the illusion that they are the capsule of wisdom and the most potent expression of this recognition is rigorous regard for the views of others. This is manifested in large part by a welcoming disposition towards difference of opinion. This welcoming disposition towards difference of opinion should not, however, be interpreted to mean that each has a right to their own facts or the creation of same. How the facts are interpreted is one thing. What the facts are, is quite another. But even on the question of what facts are relevant to a discussion is seen by the leader, who is comfortable with opposition, as collectively, rather than unilaterally, determined.

Organizational change efforts will expire quickly if the cause being pursued is personal and self-serving or when the motivation comes from some tiff that a leader wants settled or some itch that we want addressed. The first question a leader should ask therefore, when taking up a cause is, "how will what I am seeking to accomplish address the larger agenda?". If an answer cannot be found to that question, which answer is relevant to every context in which the question may be asked by others, then the capacity for endurance is suspect. Another way of making this point is simply to say, only pursue causes that will impact the larger agenda. Only in those circumstances is it likely that the cause will be capable of being subject to perseverance.

An important caution that the reimaginative leader should heed is that they should not become partisan or form cliques around themselves. It is self-evident that a cause must be seeking to shift the balance of resources or attention from one thing to the other or more equitably among various needs and interests and in that regard there must be a bias to a particular position. The cause will find fuel when the particular position is defensible as a principle, as against fighting for a person – even if what may have occasioned the fight is the treatment of a person or the interest of a person. The fuel is easily consumed and ends in thin air when the agenda is tied to a person, as Kotter (1996) suggests. The top leader in an organization who asks others to change for their sake is being as foolish and short-sighted as the leader at a lower level in the organization who makes a fight of an issue about a person instead of a principle.

Summary

The twenty-first century represents an era of rapid changes and organizations which will survive and succeed in the highly competitive global market will be those which are able to adapt their processes and products and re-align the skills of their people to respond to the rapidly changing needs. A central plank in the success of the adaptation of organizations will be the quality of leadership. For leaders to be successful in spearheading the change efforts of the organizations they lead; they need to be constructively subversive and courageous in engaging others, as well as be persevering.

CHAPTER 7

Qualities 7, 8, and 9: Care, Justice, and Trust

One of the traditional conceptions of leadership is that great leaders are tough. US President Donald Trump has given credence to that notion by his aggressive and uncompromising rhetoric. But contrary to the notions of toughness, crudeness, and the tendency to be dismissive of and disrespectful towards others is the idea that an effective leader can be gracious and compassionate yet effective. Two unquestionable tenets of the reimaginative model of leadership are care towards those we lead and a disciplined approach to building trust with those we lead.

In the data for this study, the variable which accounts for the largest variation in the behaviour of the data, as shown in table 2.2 is "demonstrate care". This suggests that team members expect that the leader will be caring and compassionate towards them. The first subfactor under demonstrating care is listening. A caring leader listens to the concerns and opinions of their team. The second variable which accounts for the behaviour of the data is "takes interest in the opinions of staff". Together, these two variables account for more than 53 per cent in the variation of the data as shown in figure 2.2. These ideas are corroborated in table 2.3 with the notion of respect added as one of the subfactors which explain the meaning of factor two which speaks to the creation of an inclusive work environment.

Carnegie (2017) counsels that people do not care how much we know until they know how much we care. The leader who demonstrates genuine care for others will soon win their respect, commitment and support. Conversely, the leader who does not take the feelings of others into account and who behaves as if they can get the job done simply by giving orders and monitoring performance rigorously, will soon find that the two most effective tools of supervision are not clear objectives and close observation but challenging objectives and caring interaction.

The expression of care or compassion must be more than about optics or political correctness, which Covey (2004) calls market ethic. Rather, expressions of care and compassion should reflect a sincere concern for the people we lead, that is character ethic, according to Covey. According to Covey, market ethic is about spin and political correctness and assumes that there is no real need to care for people or respect them as long as we can get them to think so or at least think anything they wish as long as they get the work done.

Character ethic, on the other hand, is based on the belief that we should seek to become our best selves and in being who we are, we should endeavour to care for others genuinely and sincerely using all appropriate means to communicate this to them. Character ethic is born of the ethic of love. In simple terms, the ethic of love eschews the notion that the leader's job is simply to ensure that the work gets done and obviously runs counter to the notion that leaders either love or not love those they lead. Indeed, Smith (2011) describes leadership as an ethic of care. Employees want to know that their employers care. Employees value relationships and the quality of these relationships inform, to some degree, their sense of self as well as has the potential to inform their performance.

The Ethic of Care

Feminist theorists Gilligan (1982) and Noddings (2003) may be credited with pioneering the theory of ethics of care. The term refers to ideas concerning both the nature of morality and normative ethical theory. According to ethics of care theorists, who include Burton and Dunn (1996), the construct stands in stark contrast to ethical theories that rely on principles to highlight moral actions. Burton and Dunn suggest that the construct stands in contrast to ethical theories such as Kantian deontology and utilitarianism which are principles designed to highlight morality. Ethics of care, on the other hand, seeks to promote a pragmatic and practical mode of engagement, centred around the notion of interdependence. This approach to ethics takes account of the indispensability of community and recognizes that some people are more vulnerable. Because of the fact of differential levels of vulnerability, ethics of care theorists contend that there are some members of community who deserve and should be afforded extra consideration.

An important element of the ethics of care is that it rejects the notion of absolutes and universal truths, and instead posits a particularized, contextualized and evolutionary view of human reality, with a leaning towards those who are most vulnerable.

Using the characterization of care as advanced by ethics of care theorists, within the framework of leadership, care means ensuring that voices and views within the organization or community that are normally excluded are given an opportunity to be heard. Care is the fourth sub-factor under the factor "openness" in table 2.3. I suggest that its location under "openness" means that ultimately what matters most to team members is the confidence that their team leader is open to listening to them. The willingness to listen is a posture which amounts to giving others the opportunity to be heard. The willingness to listen is by far the most visibly caring response to the concerns of others. The justification for this assertion is found in the preceding three sub-factors that define the theme of openness. The preceding three sub-factors are:

- Show willingness to accept criticism.
- Admit error when established, and
- Respond positively to staff members when there is disagreement.

The location of these sub-factors makes a compelling case for what openness and caring are about. The leader's expression of care for team members, and demonstration of interest in capacities of team members are structurally driven by the creation of conditions for staff members to participate in decision-making activities. This is buttressed by behaviours such as the willingness to admit error, the willingness to accept criticism, openness to adopting solutions proposed by team members and using approaches and ideas that emanated from them. The structural provisions of caring and interest in the contributions of others are also seen in the opportunities that are created for team members to develop their potential and capacities.

Monarth (2014) references research that has shown that helping others feel more powerful can boost productivity, improve performance, and leave employees feeling more satisfied on the job. He cites a study conducted by Yona Kifer of Tel Aviv university that found that employees were 26 per cent more satisfied in their roles when they had positions of power. Being able to make decisions or participate in decision-making contributes to feelings of power.

According to Monarth, the researchers found that feelings of power also translated to more authenticity and feelings of well-being. Power made the subjects feel more "true to themselves", enabling them to engage in actions that authentically reflected values they hold dear. This subjective sense of authenticity in turn created a higher sense of wellbeing and happiness. When a leader creates the conditions for team members to experience feelings of happiness they are perceived as showing care.

Caring for team members and showing interest in their contributions are also manifested in how the leader chooses to exercise power as against the frequency with which they rely on influencing rather than demanding compliance. Martin (2017) explains that he finds there are three things that are crucial in leading talented people. These are (a) treating them as individuals rather than as members of a class; (b) continuously providing opportunity; and (c) giving pats on the back. These actions are components of care.

The interpretation that team members make of the efforts expended by their leaders for creating the amenities and facilities for the level of engagement described above is that it boils down to an issue of justice. Thus, the leader who is committed to the range of behaviours and processes discussed is perceived as an advocate for justice.

Care is not some mushy emotional stuff, though it involves emotional sensitivity and emotional intelligence. Care is about the creation of structures and systems that meet the needs of team members. One of the greatest needs of human beings is the desire to participate in the making of decisions that affect their lives. Another important need of human beings is the desire to be challenged and through those challenges to acquire skills and competences. In this research, both involvement in decision-making and the opportunity to develop (leadership) capacities were found to be constituent elements of care and both are found to be related to perceptions of justice.

Justice Involves Facilitating Development of Others

Tables 2.6 to 2.8 in chapter two paint a picture of the notion of justice. That notion of justice, which is embedded in care, means (a) regard for the capacity of others to make a meaningful contribution and to frame their point of view, that is, not forcing one's will on another; (b) facilitating involvement in the decision-making processes of the organization; and (c) encouraging and facilitating the development of leaders at all levels in the organization.

These three components, when taken together, present justice as a process of *meaningful inclusion*. In this regard, justice is not mere presence (as being present at a meeting), it involves contending with alternative views without an attempt to use power to enforce one's will. Meaningful inclusion is not mere information transmission (as in being told what decisions have been taken); it involves consultation and debate. Neither is it mere acknowledgement (as in being recognized as a potential leader). It involves giving space and other resources to enable others to develop their leadership abilities.

Rawls (1972) defines justice as fair distribution of goods, rights and responsibilities. Ryan (2006), in critiquing Rawls, contends that Rawls's definition was limited in that it did not take account of the structures that would limit that distribution and suggested that a more helpful construction of justice is *meaningful inclusion* in organizational practices and processes.

While Ryan's critique of Rawls is contentious, the notion of *meaningful inclusion* is the most apt construction of what justice is. Distribution as constructed by Rawls suggests a chief agent distributing goods, access and rights, while inclusion suggests a collective engagement in the sharing of responsibilities and rights. It is inevitable in any organization that someone will have to lead the process of inclusion and in that leadership role, the creation of the pathways to ensure access to rights and the sharing of responsibility has to be overseen by someone with ultimate accountability. Even though all leaders share accountability, the person in the school with ultimate accountability is the principal.

Drawing on the insights that emerge from the foregoing, justice may be defined as a relational and leadership variable in which due regard is paid to the capacity of others to make a valuable contribution to the well-being and development of the group or organization. As a consequence, it involves the establishment of structures and systems to facilitate meaningful inclusion in the processes of decision-making. Once people are involved in decision-making, they will have an opportunity to ensure that their rights are protected, and their other needs are met. This protection of rights and meeting of needs include ensuring that adequate support systems exist to enable them to execute their duties and responsibilities. In circumstances in which limited resources may mean that not all their needs are met, their involvement in some of the processes of decision-making will enable them to negotiate and make informed choices.

Schriesheim and Neider (2012) in *Research in Management: Perspectives on Justice and Trust in Organizations* catalogue a series of global events that have led to the erosion of trust in leaders and suggest, that when trust is eroded it is difficult, if not impossible, for persons who are affected by the actions of leaders to perceive that justice has been done, or that they were treated fairly; even if, given the facts of the situation, the decisions taken were the correct and logical ones.

Yilmaz and Altinkurt (2012), conducted research in Turkish secondary schools and examined the relationships between organizational justice, on the one hand, and organizational trust and organizational citizenship behaviours, on the other. The study sought to determine whether, and to what extent, organizational justice and organizational trust predict variation in the organizational citizenship behaviours of teachers. They found that there was a positive and moderate level relationship between organizational citizenship, on the one hand, and organizational justice, trust in the principal, trust in colleagues, and trust in stakeholders, on the other.

While the relationship between justice and trust and the consequential behaviours are perhaps self-evident, there is a deeper question that must be asked to grasp a better understanding of this relationship. Zenger and Folkman (2014), in research which examined the differences between managing and coaching, found that the managers become effective coaches when, in their management styles, they are collaborative rather than directive; help team members to discover rather than give advice; and act as equal rather than as expert. In one of their important conclusions, they note that the most effective managers who are also effective coaches learn to be selective about giving direction. Rather than use their conversations as an opportunity to exert a strong influence, make recommendations and provide unambiguous directions, they take a step back, and try to draw out the views of their talented, experienced staff. These notions are consistent with what this study has found and articulated as the relationship between justice and influence.

The second embodiment of justice, as found in the data in chapter two, is the relationship which was found between the variables "advocate for justice", and two other variables, namely: "creating the conditions for participation in decision-making" and "allowing leaders to develop" with correlations of 0.565 and 0.405, respectively. What these relationships suggest is that teams regard involvement in decision-making not merely as a nice thing, but as a vital thing; so vital that it boils down to a question of rights. The era of the twenty-first century is likely to be the period of the *assertion* of rights in a manner far greater than the second half of the twentieth century. The second half of the twentieth century may be more properly characterized as the period of the acquiring of rights which are now being asserted in the twenty-first century.

Based on the relationship between the two variables mentioned above, it may be asserted that justice involves the development of team members. Blasé and Blasé (1999), in a study conducted in the US among a sample of 809 teachers, found that there were two major themes that defined teachers' perspectives on effective instructional leadership – "talking with teachers to promote reflection" and "promoting professional growth".

The findings and conclusions of Blasé and Blasé are consistent with the findings of the study that has informed this work. Their findings are like that of Fullan (2014), who in his book, *The Principal – Three Keys to Maximizing Impact,* identifies "change agent" as the third key to being an effective principal and lists as elements of change agency behaviours such as empowerment, listening, collaboration and support. The qualities of leadership at the epicentre of effective leadership are adumbrated in Fullan's findings.

Monarth (2014), who in citing research conducted by Yona Kifer of the University of Tel Aviv, argues that when employees are enabled to feel powerful, the feeling can boost productivity and fuel improvements in performance, thus leaving employees feeling more satisfied on the job. Monarth's argument corroborates Ouchi (1981), who argues that a major explanation for the difference in the productivity levels between Japanese and American workers was the extent to which Japanese workers are allowed to participate in the decision-making process and thus feel more powerful.

Zhang, Lin, and Fong (2012), in their regional pathbreaking work entitled, *Servant Leadership: A Preferred Style of School Leadership in Singapore,* examined changes in leadership practices and expectations in Singapore over the fifty-year period 1960–2010. They found that over the period, servant leadership had become more acceptable than authoritative leadership and that servant leadership was more effective because it reflects better use of the leaders' power. Arguing that servant leadership is driven by the philosophy of "First to serve and then to lead", the authors also found that staff experienced higher levels of motivation when exposed to servant leadership.

Hutton (2011) has also made findings that are consistent with the general body of literature advanced above. Hutton sought to determine the qualities of effective principals and uncovered nine key qualities. Hutton used a qualitative methodology and interviewed twenty principals and the regional directors of the Ministry of Education in Jamaica. The third of the nine qualities of effective principals uncovered by Hutton is that "high performing (effective) principals provide leadership that is visionary, engaging, passionate, visible, and demanding but they always depend on the collective energy of the staff".

The issue of collective energy points to the fact that the performance of the school is not the result of a lone super-star but a team of committed players. Relying on the literature on collective leadership, it has been noted (Thompson 2009) that there is a groundswell of opposition to the lone-leader approach to school leadership. Any leader who thinks they can single-handedly turn around a school is either being dishonest or naïve.

A number of other studies have contributed to the debate on leadership involving the development of others (Leithwood, Harris and Hopkins 2008; Heck and Hallinger 2009; Murphy et al. 2007; and Darling-Hammond, Wei and Andree 2010). The main elements of effectiveness identified suggest that an effective principal sets a clear strategic direction – for both instructional and organizational development, supports and develops people, and creates the parameters for improving student performance.

The central question of how this is done is connected to the issue of the sharing of leadership. The question of the sharing of leadership invites us to examine the larger questions of how widely leadership should be distributed and what are teachers' expectations of how the principal should lead and what should be the breadth and depth of the sharing of leadership.

Reimagining Succession Planning and Developing Others

Byham (2012), in a useful article entitled *Taking Your Succession Management Plan into the 21st Century,* discusses a few mistakes that organizations make in their succession planning efforts. Among these errors he includes:
- Focusing people's development on specific jobs and
- No ongoing support and reinforcement by senior management.

There are several fundamental facts that must inform succession planning. These include: (a) The biological reality that as human beings mature (and age) our energies and capacities diminish. A two-year-old will tire her mom, and a twelve-year-old not only learns faster than a fifty-year-old but runs faster. (b) Given the direction of global demographics, organizations will increasingly have to rely upon the skills of mature workers and will have to do so for periods that may be longer than anticipated. These two facts mean that for organizations to be successful they will have to ensure that their investments in the development of workers are so distributed as to enable the organization to draw the returns from those investments over a longer period and across a wider range of developmental changes.

Given what is known about millennials, particularly in respect of their expectation of rapid progression and recognition and given what the research has shown about what workers expect, organizations will need to be more reimaginative and creative in designing their succession planning systems. Based on the data and the direction of the literature, three approaches to succession planning for businesses are warranted.

1. Organizations must train and appoint teams of persons to succeed to higher positions, as against training and appointing an individual. Thus, rather than having a chief executive officer, there are two chief executive officers who work collaboratively. It is often said that the job of a CEO can be lonely. Part of that loneliness results from the fact that in making certain decisions the CEO must consult with themselves only. In the same way that a committee may have co-chairs

why cannot an organization have co-presidents?

2. Term limits should be introduced for all employees (not just senior employees). Part of the reason millennials desire rapid progression is their low threshold for boredom. Organizations could meet this need by building into their organizations' modus operandi, a system of mandatory job change after a given period. Such a system would also play well with millennials who are generally multi-skilled. This system could include returning to previous positions held.

3. A system of mandatory exits from the organization after five to ten years should be implemented. Given that pensions have been made portable since the 1990s in many countries, employees need not fear loss of pension benefits if they are required to resign from an organization after ten years. In this way the organization will be able to continuously renew itself with fresh talent. There is also an advantage in this approach for employees. By making resignation mandatory after ten years, employees are likely to be less anxious about underhanded ways being used to stimulate turnover and by knowing their exit date, subject only to factors such as organizational closure or termination for cause, employees can plan their lives with greater care or strategy.

The foregoing approach frees the organizations from having to wait for some future date for workers to begin to show and use the various skills that they have acquired. Instead, senior management must place upon itself the obligation of putting in place the support systems that make it possible for the newly learned and emerging skills to be articulated. Thus, while succession planning in an age when the demographic pyramid is turned on its head will require that skills learned be relevant for longer periods, it is also necessary that their engagement and utilization occur early. Of course, there is also the imperative of ensuring that there is continuous learning. Ultimately then, the process of succession planning while taking account of replacement of workers will, in a demographically changed era, involve more continuation of skill use.

The Issue of Trust

Trust is vital to every valued relationship and is one of the most critical assets of a leader (Rezaei, Salehi, Shafiei and Sabet 2012). Molm (2003) argues that the issue of distrust is a major contributor to problems such as employee withdrawal, lack of commitment and employee underperformance. Indeed, one of the inevitable imperatives of effective leadership is that of inspiring and winning the trust of others (Thompson 2018c).

Trust is not just a belief in something that lies outside of oneself, rather it is generated and understood through language, emotions and relationships. Trust emerges when there is a sense that a leader cares. According to Blanchard (2010) who outlines what he calls an ABCD trust model, trust is synonymous with care. The third component of that model is connectedness, which Blanchard describes as demonstrating care. The other components of Blanchard's trust model are ability, believability, and dependability. Other factors have been posited (Thompson 2018c), which nurture organizational trust namely: trusting in the collective wisdom of staff, encouraging diversity of perspectives, willingness to debate issues in situations where opinions differ, being a good listener, promoting collective responsibility, and responding positively to staff members when there is disagreement.

Leman and Pentak (2004) using the metaphor of the leader as a shepherd, explain the concept of developing trust-building, using the acronym SHAPE, and argue that a caring leader, like a good shepherd, knows the shape of his sheep. This means knowing the **S**trengths of members of the team; knowing their **H**earts and what motivates them; paying attention to their **A**ttitudes and the things to which they are prone to respond negatively or positively; knowing their **P**ersonality, their likes and dislikes, their idiosyncrasies; knowing their **E**xperiences – the gifts, painful memories and possibly unresolved issues they bring to the context of work. Mills-Schofield (2012) in describing the most important lessons she has learnt from her bosses includes the demonstration of a deep consciousness that employees are humans. She laments that many companies treat their employees as employees – nicely and kindly, even generously – but not as humans, and contrasted her own experience noting that her manager-mentors made it clear that she mattered not just for what she could do, but also for who she was. Many bosses have come to know repeatedly that they "get" far more out of employees whom they treat with tenderness and genuine care than out of those whom they simply regard as just being a worker even when they treat them with respect and professional regard.

This issue of tenderness is similar to what Leman and Pentak describe as "knowing the shape of your sheep" and "taking time to tend their hoofs". Even though beasts of the forest, by instinct, show tenderness to their own, it is a decidedly human quality, infused perhaps with divine ingredients, when as human beings we show tenderness towards each other. One of the sharply contested issues in the 2012 US presidential election was which of the presidential candidates was able to show more empathy and who had displayed a greater capacity for tenderness and care. The reimaginative leader knows that they touch another deeply when they can be touched by their pain.

Summary

The type of leadership that is appropriate for the twenty-first century is one that is caring and focused on building trust. Care and trust require the pursuit of justice, and justice involves, among other things, giving employees a voice not only by listening to their opinions and concerns but in creating space for them to bring their expertise to bear on the decision-making processes of the organization.

PART THREE
Applications of Reimaginative Leadership Qualities

In this section, four contexts of leadership are examined which show practical applications of the leadership qualities the qualities of reimaginative leadership. The experiences of two schools are reviewed and the story of a successful Jamaican company, Jamaica Money Market Brokers, as told by an executive of the company, is explored. An analysis of the philosophy and management practices of the American multinational, the 3M company is presented together with the insights of the lives of seven globally recognized leaders are presented. Purposively chosen, these characters lived in different time periods, came from vastly different backgrounds, had different professions, came from different countries, and possessed somewhat different faith orientations, but had four things in common: their daring courage, they challenged the status quo, they did not occupy positions of officialdom when they made their marks on history, and they changed the contexts of their time for generations. Beyond those four common qualities, there are many others which each possessed as can be evidenced from their personal stories, but which also can be tested by examining the broader details of their lives. The convergence of the experiences across schools, business and individuals underscores the essence of reimaginative leadership.

CHAPTER 8
Alternatives-Thinking, Trust-Building, and Risk-Taking in Two Jamaican Schools

Thompson, Burke, King, and Wong (2017) explore the experiences of two schools that experienced reimaginative renewal. Elements of the stories of these two schools are captured here to illustrate how the approaches used by both principals moved their schools from the ranks of underperforming to being high performing schools. The schools were pseudo-named Oasis High and Seaview High.

Among the strategies that were employed by the principals to achieve turnaround of their schools were:

1. conveying to the students and staff that there was an alternative to how they were performing and being perceived as an institution;
2. building strong relationships;
3. modelling the behaviours expected of others, and
4. demonstrating courage in taking risks in pursuit of goals.

Communicating That There Were Alternatives

Reimagining how any institution may perform and transcend itself requires leadership that is focused on changing the status quo based on an audacious vision of a better future. The principals articulated the view that their success depended on the extent to which they could communicate and gain buy-in for a compelling and audacious vision for their schools, located in the belief that how things were needed not be how they remained. Both schools had poor public reputations and were ranked among low-performing schools. The principals were also mindful that they would likely face strong opposition, at least from some stakeholders. Mindful of this, both principals saw their first task as crafting and selling that bold new vision while being willing to take on their would-be opponents. They reckoned that in the long run a culture shift was non-negotiable.

The principal for Oasis High was somewhat abrasive but also displayed a greater urgency and at times impolite impatience when naysayers and opponents were perceived as standing in his way, and on a few occasions was so abrasive towards students that his actions became the subject of legal challenge. These situations did not, however, deter him in his pursuit to create a culture in which all stakeholders shared certain core values and beliefs about schooling. Seaview's principal had similar instances in which he had to forcibly enforce rules without negotiation or latitude given for exceptions.

There were similar situations in which staff members would violate rules concerning punctuality for the start of the school day and arrival at classes, timely submission of grades and dress deemed appropriate. While some members of staff were willingly compliant some were passively resistant. Both principals reported that they had to take strong measures to ensure full compliance as the status quo, though repulsive to some, was being enjoyed by others.

Both principals expressed an awareness of the need for the collective will for transformation to be sold through constructive engagement, but they also took the view that at the pace at which change was warranted there was not a lot of time to wait until everyone was on board willingly. They contended that while both students and teachers who resisted the new culture may have found it difficult to cope, their ability to display the acceptable behaviours would soon come naturally, once they are pressured into doing the right thing long enough.

Building Strong Relationships

A central pillar of one principal's "winning" strategy was the building of strong relationships with stakeholders at all levels. This principal indicated that the philosophy that undergirded this was his "motivation, elevation and inspiration" strategy. This strategy he said was necessary in order to keep spirits high and enable members of staff and students to believe in themselves. This belief in self he considered to be a central pillar of strong relationships. The principal sought to give expression to this philosophy by creating work teams or committees which were given defined deliverables. Each of these work teams or committees would be led by a different staff member. This strategy was not only designed to build and strengthen relationships, it was also designed to build a culture of distributive leadership, shared ownership and mutual accountability, as well as building leadership capacities at all levels of the organization.

Seaview was located in an area in which it is the only community asset of its kind in the immediate environs. As a consequence, its profile and performance received significant attention from the community. The major institutions and businesses in the community, as well as the members of the public, were reported to have expressed great disappointment with the school – both staff and students. To be a student at Seaview High during the period of the school's ravaged public reputation was a guarantee that once in uniform, members of the public (be they passengers on buses or shoppers in the local businesses) would stand clear of them, sometimes in fear. There were stories of students entering people's property to steal, maim animals and terrify residents.

Given the school's uncomplimentary record, business leaders were of the view that the school was simply not the kind of place in which to invest. The consequence of the lack of support from the community meant that the school was limited in how much it could do, given that the Ministry of Education provided support mainly for salaries. As a result, the principal had to invest heavily in building stakeholder relations. Among other things, he visited businesses and met with owners and shared with them his philosophy, his vision and his plans for the school which included specific performance targets. Through his initiatives at building stronger community relations, he was able to garner community support. This support contributed to the percentage of students sitting external exams moving from forty-three per cent in 2013 to ninety-four per cent in 2015.

Modelling the Behaviours Desired from Others

The principals understood that they could not ask their staff to commit to standards of service and performance which they, as principals, did not display. Thus, both principals saw the need to visibly demonstrate the level of urgency, commitment, respect for self and others, accountability and responsibility that they required of staff and students. Seaview's principal emphasized that he held himself to the strictest standards of accountability in all respects – punctuality, time management, efficiency, deportment, interpersonal relationships, and the respect he showed to students. He explained that there was never a time when he was complacent; he saw goals as ever changing and encouraged both students and staff to "always raise the bar".

One principal recalled that during the first half of his first year there was a high level of unpunctuality and absence. In response, he introduced both punitive and positive measures including disciplinary letters which he publicly committed to escalate to dismissals. The result of these measures was that for the academic year 2014–15 he had almost perfect attendance and punctuality from both staff and students. He attributed the improvements in attendance and punctuality to the fact that staff members began to see themselves differently.

The other principal emphasized that his showing respect and regard for students and treating them as ladies and gentlemen were major components of his attempt to model for the teachers how he expected them to treat students. He also contended that this approach had the effect of encouraging students to see themselves differently. Both the way the principal chose to address students and the responses that were seen in their behaviour began to alter the school's climate, he asserted.

Demonstrating Courage in Taking Risks in Pursuit of Goals

An underperforming school typically faces a range of complex problems for which there are rarely defined protocols for resolution. As such the management of those problems requires creativity, thinking out of the box and risk-taking. These perspectives were articulated by both principals. In one principal's view, it was his thinking outside the box, which more than any other variable explained the progress and success his school experienced. It was his willingness to go where others had not gone and to do what others would be afraid of doing. He asserted that risk-taking primarily involves taking unconventional routes which are often faster and more efficient in seeking to produce noble and necessary results, which while probably achievable through conventional routes, were subject to the greater risk of not being achieved.

One of the prerequisites for risk-taking that the other principal articulated was that of being willing to stand on one's own and to face whatever consequences may result if the decision to go the unconventional route backfired. Both principals recognized the enormous importance of risk-taking and exercised a level of determination in the face of opposition. Piccolo (2005) establishes that there is a relationship between innovation and risk-taking and reflects the wisdom of one of the principals who argues that all decisions have some level of risk – whether one decides to act or not to act. Thus, he argued, that the astute leader must weigh the risks and decide on the risk they are prepared to take. If one is successful in making high-value, risky decisions that produce good results, one's moral authority is expanded, and one is therefore given more leeway to take high-stakes decisions. Such high-stakes decisions could be as complex as taking a student in his car and taking that student home to his parents, given the probability that the parents may not be home, but the gains made in terms of social capital and trust between the parents and the school, if they were at home, to receive their child and have a conversation with the principal about the child's future would be worth the risk.

The route of risk-taking for the Seaview principal was not reported in as philosophical a manner as his counterpart, perhaps because he was a much longer serving veteran and understood the importance of measured disclosures, even to researchers. One of the main risks reported by him was his refusal to give up on students who had been written off by some of their teachers, and by sticking with them and creating opportunities for their development and finding that, in a good number of cases, their performance exceeded expectation.

One school experienced the fruits of the turnaround efforts within the first year of the principal's incumbency. The evidence of the turnaround was seen in several key areas. In the area of student discipline, the number of suspensions fell sharply from 125 in 2013, the first year to 87 in 2014, a thirty per cent decline and then to 5 in 2015, a phenomenal ninety-five per cent decline. Similar spectacular changes were evident during the first year at the other school, particularly in student discipline. Within two weeks of his arrival there was significant improvement in student punctuality and a massive reduction in dress code violations moving from 376 in the school year 2011–12 to 17 in school year 2014–15.

Themes from the Stories of the Two Schools

The themes emerging from the stories of these schools show, in the first place, that a principal tasked with the responsibility of turning around an underperforming school must be skilled in the art of managing resistance. The chief tool in the management of resistance used by the principals was by seeking to engage everyone. This approach is consistent with the principles of reimaginative leadership.

Effecting change requires persistence and courageous perseverance. The persistence that will be required in managing resistance to efforts at turning around an underperforming school will have to be buttressed by the strategic use of data. By relying on data, the principals created a forum for staff to bring their experience in the school and their technical expertise in interpreting the data. Data tell the story of a school's reality but what stories are told and how the stories are told will depend on who is included in the telling of the stories; that is the interpretation of the data.

A further theme present in the story of these schools is a combination of lessons which confirm the elements of reimaginative leadership namely that: (1) the credibility of the leader's call to staff for a higher level of performance rests on the extent to which the leader embodies the behaviours that others are called upon to display; and (2) the perceptions that staff and students have of themselves and how they can be inspired to have other self-perceptions. These behaviours reflect the reimaginative leadership qualities of mutual accountability and influence, specifically inspiration.

CHAPTER 9
Solutions-Orientation, Trust, and Mutual Accountability at Jamaica Money Market Brokers Ltd

Brief History and Core Beliefs of JMMB

Jamaica Money Market Brokers Ltd. (JMMB) was founded in 1992 by the late Joan Duncan. The company was founded on the values of love, care, openness, excellence in client care, honesty and integrity. According to the Donna Duncan, daughter of Joan Duncan, Joan saw every human being as possessing the capacity to show love and to manifest greatness. These core values shape and are reflected in the company's vision of love. Joan reimagined the idea of leadership and the idea of a company.

JMMB is a pioneering securities brokerage house based on participative leadership. The company operates on the belief that leadership can be and is expressed at every level and is not dependent on position. This world view is entirely consistent with that of reimaginative leadership which holds that leadership is a behaviour, not a position.

A core element of the company's belief system is the obligation of team members to act in the best interest of all. This belief undergirds the company's "Vision of Love" charter. The company holds the view that the showing of love for others (team members and customers), is consistent with the reimaginative leadership principles of trust and mutual accountability. Love requires trust and the actions of one to another (whom ones loves) will take account a sense of duty to both self and the other.

JMMB's commitment to the "Vision of Love" is epitomized in its cultural shaping practices. All employees undergo training in the principles of love, and the importance placed on this undertaking is reflected in the fact that it is led from the highest level by a senior executive responsible for cultural and human development.

Solutions-Orientation through Conversations for Greatness

A central feature of the mode of JMMB's solutions-orientation is its "Conversations for Greatness" programme, in which it engages employees and citizens, (particularly children) in conceptualizing and pursuing actions which can lead to greater personal and group success and well-being.

JMMB's leadership model which emphasizes love as a core principle and a family culture (among staff and between staff and customers) encased in a warm and welcoming environment or climate, is deliberate about giving space for ideas to contend. Indeed, the predicate of the company's solutions-orientation framework, "Conversations for Greatness" is the giving of space for ideas to contend. The creation of space for staff, and members of the communities within which JMMB operates, to share ideas and commit to actions and behaviours informed by common positions arising from those conversations, creates the foundation for mutual accountability. This strategy of conversation as a tool for designing shared solutions, achieves the ends of also promoting trust and mutual accountability.

Donna Duncan acknowledged that the practice of mutual accountability requires developing a healthy appetite for opposing views. In the absence of such an appetite, people shut down and become disengaged. When an organization's culture acquires the capacity for healthy engagement with opposing views, it is better able to undertake authentic and difficult conversations and evolves from one-dimensional reiterations of what is, to contemplating wide-ranging and complex possibilities.

As Chief Cultural and Development Officer, Duncan recognizes that in her attempts to lead cultural change, she had to display the behaviours she wanted to see in others. This acknowledgement is consistent with the Thompson's (2019b) Proposition MRM. Proposition MRM refers to modelling, respect, and motivation, which are the three variables which Thompson found to be the most defining expectations that followers had of leaders. In relation modelling, Thompson's argument is that leaders have a duty to embody in their behaviours and relationships, the standards, and practices they expected of followers. In modelling the behaviours expected of others, a leader not only creates the framework for mutual accountability, but also opens the path for attention to be paid to the greater good. That greater good, however an organization may define or interpret it at a given time, defines the purpose for which the organization exists.

Duncan shares that one of the ways in which she challenged herself to grow was to focus on the greater good. This she said involves transcending, which required that she freed self from the self-entrapment and persevere putting the greater good ahead of my personal convenience. She concluded that the degree of transformation realized is matched to the degree of transcendence of the ego and the ego trappings and the courage one is willing to show.

There are several attributes of the construct of reimaginative leadership which resonate with the JMMB way of viewing and practising leadership. Donna Duncan identified these to include: Openness to debate

i. Willingness to challenge the status quo.
ii. The authority of collective wisdom
iii. "Higher good of the organization"
iv. "Everyone brings value and each one's contribution is vital"
v. Learning from each experience
vi. Seeking to understand the other person's world
vii. Solutions orientation
viii. Taking responsibility for and acknowledging when a mistake is made. (Joan Duncan was quick to remind teams of the fact that "pencils are made with rubbers".)
ix. Resolving conflicts by genuinely sharing feelings and interpretations, to have nothing unsaid and to maintain authentic relationships.

Human Resource Management and Engagement

The foregoing principles are infused in JMMB's selection process. When selecting leaders the company makes it very clear to potential employees that the company's culture does not support a hierarchical organization but one based on equity and equality, thus leaders have to be open to being held accountable by anyone in the organization. Duncan reiterates that JMMB holds to the view that leaders exist at all levels of the organization, although different leaders have different types of accountabilities. While each leader is subject to accountability, each performs an important role in providing leadership in the company.

Duncan emphasizes that the principle of mutual accountability is not just a philosophical construct at JMMB, arguing that an important element of mutual accountability is taking ownership. Towards this end, she noted that the practice of taking ownership is reinforced by way of an ESOP (Employee Share Ownership Plan) wherein all employees are owners of the company.

Duncan asserts that JMMB attributes its phenomenal success to its embrace of the principles of reimaginative leadership, arguing that throughout the company's thirty years of existence, it has sought to operationalize those principles and has realized great results. She notes that genuine care for clients and the maintenance of low corporate margins (high returns) to clients led to unprecedented growth in our client base – higher than any other brokerage house in the Caribbean. She concludes that the reimaginative leadership framework captures key elements of what the company has found to be essential to live true to our vision on a day-to-day basis.

She explains that the company's success also relates to the fact that it has three bottom lines. (1) That team members must realize their dreams and their greatness, (2) that customers realize their dreams and their greatness, and (3) that shareholders to benefit from that. Thus, she emphasizes that the financial bottom line is only one of three bottom lines. This approach to leadership places people at the centre, she contends, and given the demands and pressures of fast-paced economies and societies it gets harder and harder to maintain a sustainable competitive advantage, unless organizations have people who are inspired, who will take initiative, whose personal values and vision are aligned with the company's values and vision, and who are working together for the greater good and for the best interest of all. She concludes by affirming that reimaginative leadership provides a framework for leaders to guide leaders in being able to achieve this end.

CHAPTER 10
Alternatives-Thinking, Inspiration, and Innovation at the 3M Company (USA)

The 3M company's philosophy is a compelling expression on reimaginative leadership. The 2019 version of the company's website homepage displays the words "Celebrate the power of curiosity, passion, and purpose" and the tagline under these words states tersely "wonder with us". The organizational policies and practices behind these words confirm that 3M is a company which embraces the elements of reimaginative leadership as outlined in this book, namely: alternatives-thinking, courage, empowerment, influence, inspiration, mutual accountability, and subversion.

Originally known as the Minnesota Mining and Manufacturing Company, 3M is a large multinational organization based in the United States of America. The company is involved in the manufacturing of a wide range of business and consumer goods in the fields of automotive, electronics, industrial safety, health care, office supplies, and personal protective equipment, among others. The company manufactures over fifty thousand products ranging from its famous and renowned Post-it® notes and Scotch® Tape to transdermal patches of nitroglycerin and a prescription cream for treating genital warts. The company was founded in 1902 and has subsidiaries in Canada, India, and Japan, and operations in over sixty countries. In 2018, the company had over ninety-three thousand employees, was worth over US$31billion, and was ranked as the one hundred and tenth largest company in the US.

Perhaps the singular and most defining characteristic of 3M is its commitment to, and long track record in, promoting innovation and interdepartmental cooperation. In support of its culture of innovation, the company invests over US$1 billion annually to support research, and in 2003, one year after its one hundredth anniversary, realigned its operations into seven major business units – Consumer and Office; Display and Graphics; Electro and Communications; Health Care; Industrial; Safety, Security, and Protection Services; and Transportation. The volume of resources invested in research reflects a policy commitment of nurturing independent thinking. Independent thinking is the germ of which alternatives-thinking is made. Interdepartmental cooperation within a context of robust independent thinking requires, and is made possible through, empowerment, influence, and inspiration.

Alternatives-Thinking, Empowerment, and the Story of Post-it®

The 3M Company's commitment to innovation is exemplary. It has been argued that organizations which innovate are likely to be more successful than those which do not (Popa, Preda, and Boldea n.d.). The contention is that organizations which dispose of the necessary resources to ensure innovation send a powerful motivation to employees and this level of commitment shapes the organizational climate and empowers team members to exercise the courage to explore innovative ideas. Innovation is, perhaps, the most formidable expression of alternatives-thinking. When alternatives-thinking is embraced as the fundamental quality of leadership there is an inherent assumption that the organization must simultaneously give space and power for people to imagine, for people to "think outside the box", for people to wonder aloud, for people to ask "why?"

People empowerment is not achieved merely by establishing structures that provide for more persons to occupy management positions. People empowerment begins with the creation and fostering of a culture that encourages differences of opinion, nurtures intellectual diversity, and rewards those who are courageous and daring enough to take a different path, to tackle difficult problems and in the end produce superior results. This approach to alternatives-thinking and empowerment underlie innovation at 3M and provide the backdrop for one of its earliest world renown products, Post-it ®.

It is also to be reckoned that the practice of true people empowerment, which often expresses itself in rewarding those who achieve spectacular results outside the regular paths, does not mean that when spectacular results are not immediately forthcoming, or when there are errors, people are ignored or punished. A people-empowering culture in fact gives space for people to make errors and encourages learning from errors. This giving of space to err is what lies behind the history of the world-famous Post-it paper. The harmless adhesive on the paper is the product of an experiment that "failed". The innovator, an employee at the 3M Company, had set out to create a particular type of glue. The glue that resulted from the experiment turned out not to be sticky enough and so, consistent with the company's non-waste policy, the employee had to find another use for the glue. Thus "Post-it" was invented.

In addition to the support for alternatives-thinking and empowerment, expressed in vast amounts of resources invested in research at 3M, employees are rewarded for their innovation. Employees who create inventions receive a percentage of the global sales of the product for a defined period. More importantly they receive recognition and earn the authority and confidence that come with being an inventor. Thus, at the heart of innovation is the will to imagine and this imagination is what has contributed vastly to 3M's massive line of products.

Innovation, Inspiration, Influence, and Subversion

Innovation cannot be taught or made the subject of policy, rather people must generate the will and desire to innovate. Innovation is not merely doing a job; it represents the approach that one takes to doing a job. Innovation is a by-product or out-growth of alternatives-thinking and at 3M, the success and progress of employees are predicated on their willingness to innovate. Such an approach represents the individual's unique personality. In this regard, an organization which seeks to promote innovation among its employees must opt to influence and inspire the innovative disposition, it cannot dictate or command it. The approach taken at 3M is to encourage, nurture and reward innovation by, among other things, creating a non-threatening environment concerning errors and providing funding for testing and experimentation. Thus, the creation of a culture of innovation goes hand in hand with inspiration and influence, both of which are fundamental concepts and principles of reimaginative leadership.

Innovation has also been associated with terms such as "revolutionary", "disruptive", "irregular" and "discovery". Anthony (2013) discusses these concepts and highlights the concept of disruption in discussing the idea of disruptive innovation. The concept of "disruptive innovation" was coined by Harvard professor and Innosight cofounder Clayton Christensen, who describes it as a process by which a product or service takes root initially in simple applications at the bottom of a market and then relentlessly moves up the market, eventually displacing established competitors.

The alignment of the concept of 'disruption' with innovation is consistent with the reimaginative leadership principle of constructive subversion. A major explanation for the wide range of products which 3M produces is found in the fact that employees are constantly looking for ways to create new uses for existing products, thereby constructively subverting or recreating the product, and by extension the organization. In this regard therefore, constructive subversion becomes a way of life, a culture.

Power-Sharing, Inspiration, and Mutual Accountability

A company culture that emphasizes and encourages innovation is planting seeds of continuous renewal and positioning itself into a new future. Culture is created by consensus, and in an organization, this is made possible by the willingness of employees to embrace the beliefs and expected norms of the organization and express those norms and beliefs in behaviour. The 3M company reports that departmental cooperation is central to its effectiveness. Real cooperation, like respect for another person, is not something which can be coerced or mandated, it can only be evoked or influenced. The underlying quality which makes cooperation possible, particularly in instances like at 3M where there are clearly defined strategic business units, is the willingness to share power.

Cooperation between and among organizational business units cannot occur merely between and among the people at the top. For true cooperation to exist the attitudes which make this possible must be embedded in the culture of the organization and thus the voluntary behaviours of people in the organization. Cooperation requires that parties give up and share, even as they leverage power and resources. The capacity of people to share power requires courage and a sense of freedom both of which are born of the feeling of being inspired. Thus power-sharing and inspiration go hand in hand and both, which are key elements of the culture at 3M are core concepts in the art of reimaginative leadership.

A culture of cooperation is rooted in a mindset which embraces the notion of mutual accountability. Wood, Jr and Winston (2005) define leader accountability as the leader's willing acceptance of the responsibilities inherent in the leadership position with the commitment to use that position to advance the interests of the organization. They further suggest that accountability involves the willingness of the leader to provide explanations to their constituents on their beliefs, decisions, and commitments. The constituents to whom the notion of accounting is important is often understood to be governors, shareholders, and customers.

It is not often reckoned that among constituents to whom a leader must account are those they lead. In the context of an organization, constituents include persons in relation to whose performance the leader exercises supervisory powers. The concept of mutual accountability then, refers to the willingness of a leader to subject themselves to the queries and concerns of those they lead, as though those others were their boss. Thus, the basic metric of mutual accountability is the disposition to have one's performance held up for scrutiny in the same way that one scrutinizes the performance of others.

The culture of cooperation at 3M is a model of mutual accountability. Managers and their teams from different business units submit themselves to scrutiny by their peers and superiors but do so in supportive and facilitatory ways. Thus, in many respects the culture of cooperation is a form of growth and productivity facilitation.

The key concepts of reimaginative leadership focus on growth and improved productivity, with the concept productivity meaning being able to achieve more with less. The invitation to team members to engage in alternatives-thinking will ultimately result in personal and professional growth as the process results in an expansion of the mind. The empowerment of team members is not an end but a means to the end of growth and increased productivity. This agenda of empowerment requires, as 3M's experience has shown, the provision of substantial resources to fund and fuel the pursuit of the innovative undertakings which the empowerment creates. Inspiration is a seed of faith and confidence planted in the minds of others, designed to lead them to believe in their capacity to do and to exercise the courage to do.

CHAPTER 11

Alternatives-Thinking, Reliance on Influence Rather Than Power, and Trust-Building in Restoring the Jamaican Economy

Introduction

The 2008 global recession hurt the Jamaican economy badly. In 2009, the economy experienced negative growth of -3.4 per cent. In that same year, the government of Jamaica signed an agreement with the International Monetary Fund (IMF) which it failed to honour. This placed Jamaica on a path to unprecedented economic challenge, wherein the country was unable to do business with, or receive support from, major international financial entities such as the World Bank or the European Union.

The December 2011 general elections brought about a change of government in 2012, the new government commenced what would be an arduous task of rebuilding relations with the IMF and other financial institutions. An agreement was finally signed between Jamaica and the IMF in 2013, and that agreement laid the platform for a period of economic stability that continued until 2020 when the COVID-19 pandemic struck. This achievement of macro-economic stability, which began in 2013, represented a phenomenal turnaround. The person who led this process was Peter Phillips, Minister of Finance in the Portia Simpson Miller administration of 2012–16.

In assessing the process and results of the turnaround, reimaginative leadership was undoubtedly significantly responsible for what Jamaica under Phillips's leadership was able to accomplish. This chapter explores the story of Jamaica's economic turnaround partly through the eyes of Phillips, to determine if the qualities of reimaginative leadership were used and if so which of those qualities. The chapter is largely a lightly edited representation of an interview with Phillips, which was conducted in March 2020.

Wigglesworth (2020), traces the economic history of Jamaica over the forty-year period between 1973 and 2013, noting that the country had experienced forty years of anaemic economic growth, had been through periods of crises and fiscal incontinence, was highly indebted, had high levels of poverty and crime, and was being propped up by international development institutions. The World Bank characterizes Jamaica's journey starting in 2013 as an ambitious reform programme to stabilize the economy, reduce debt, and fuel growth, gaining national and international support. Charles (2019) chronicles the journey of Jamaica's economic turnaround from 2013 when, according to her, but corroborated elsewhere, including by Phillips, the then People's National Party Administration laid the foundations for what began to bear fruit in 2015. The successes which began in 2015 continued through to, and were built upon, into 2020. Further corroboration of the assertions of Charles were found in the words of former governor of the Bank of Jamaica Brian Wynter, whom she quoted from her 2019 interview with him saying: "What we've seen over the last five, six, seven years are things that nobody thought you could tackle."

One of the major things which the country tackled was its high level of indebtedness. On the question of the country's indebtedness, Jamaica's Finance Minister Nigel Clarke, writing in the *Financial Times* in February 2019 noted that in 2013, Jamaica's debt to GDP ratio was 147 per cent. Four years earlier in 2009, Clarke noted, the debt to GDP ratio was 124 per cent. This growth by twenty-three percentage points or eighteen per cent in four years represented a deadly movement in the wrong direction. Thus, as Clarke concluded, despite Jamaica securing an agreement with the IMF in 2009, and embarking on a local debt exchange, fiscal restraint could not be delivered and the agreement with the IMF collapsed.

Trust Deficit

With the agreement with the IMF collapsing in 2010 and the relationship between Jamaica and the United States of America weakening, on account of the response of the government of Jamaica to the extradition request of the US Government of the international drug kingpin Christopher Coke, there was a massive trust deficit between Jamaica and the US. By 2012, despite the eventual extradition of Coke in 2010, this trust deficit had worsened, relations having not been salvaged in the remaining years of the Orrette 'Bruce' Golding/Andrew Holness administration which ended in December 2011.

Thus the platform on which the Simpson-Miller administration began its relationship with the IMF was exceedingly shaky and according to Wigglesworth, the unofficial policy of the IMF, at least as the Jamaican government understood it, was that Jamaica should be allowed to "crash" as that was the only way that the country would "come to its senses". Wigglesworth notes that the tortuous negotiation meetings between Jamaica and the IMF would begin with the grim joke "Has Jamaica crashed yet?"

Another consequence of the trust deficit was the draconian conditions which the IMF insisted upon before it was prepared to sign an agreement with Jamaica. These conditions included a primary surplus of 7.5 per cent, a twenty-five percent increase on the 6 per cent which was in the collapsed agreement, and which was never met. To achieve this target, which was more stringent than what the IMF had demanded of Greece, there had to be a public sector wage freeze, massive tax increases, and cuts to social services. Under the leadership of Phillips, the targets were not only met, but Jamaica became a model of how to achieve economic turnaround. This turnaround does not mean, as Phillips argues in the interview, that Jamaica is now paradise; there is a lot more work that needs to be done.

Reimaginative Leadership Qualities

Phillips identifies five qualities of reimaginative leadership which he suggests have informed his leadership approach. These qualities are alternatives-thinking, the use of influence rather than power to produce results, building and maintaining trustful relationships, demonstration of care, and commitment to social justice. The quality of alternatives-thinking was deployed mainly to address the problem of low trust which existed not only between the government of Jamaica and the IMF, but also between the government and citizens, as Clarke (2019) notes. One major contributor to this low level of trust was that under previous agreements, targets would be 'met' through moving funds and resources around without attaining improvements. To counter this problem, Phillips set up the Economic Programme Oversight Committee (EPOC). The EPOC was designed as a monitoring mechanism, co-chaired by a member from the Private Sector Organisation of Jamaica (PSOJ) and the members would have full and free access to the government's books to verify that the targets were being met. The EPOC model is now an internationally recognized tool for economic oversight, trust-building, and transparency.

The quality of using influence rather than power to produce results was a vital necessity, according to Phillips. The threat of civil unrest was highly probable given the stringent measures which were imposed on the country, and the effects these had on the wages and benefits of public sector workers. In this regard, winning the confidence and support of trade unions was essential. The fact is the unions could not be commandeered into accepting the decisions of the government and there was always the risk that public sector workers could be mobilized into becoming fiercely opposed to the proposed economic programme. It was therefore imperative that the government win the confidence and support of the unions which could not be done using power. The twin qualities of demonstration of care and social justice worked hand in hand, according to Phillips.

The support of the trade unions was a precondition for the IMF signing off on the Jamaica programme; getting that initial support while pivotal for the commencement of that agreement, was equally necessary as sustaining that support. Sustaining that support required that public sector workers and the private sector had the assurance that the programme would be more than just the manipulation of numbers. This is where the role of EPOC was central. Sustaining national support also meant that vulnerable citizens felt that their concerns were understood, and pursuant to this, one provision in the programme was the setting of a floor level for financing social programmes.

The critical importance of influence as a tool for producing results is seen in the fact that when the Jamaican government faced obstacles in getting an agreement with the IMF, the government had to resort to seeking the support of influential US persons in the US administration and the Congress, as well as among connected US citizens who lived in Jamaica. The levers of power were not at the disposal of the Jamaican government.

The juxtaposition of reliance on influence rather than power to win support among Jamaican citizens, particularly public sector workers, as well as among connected US persons to secure an accepted IMF deal highlights two important lessons. In the first place it exposes the myth that it is only people in financially powerful positions that a government or the executive of an organization needs to get things done. In the story of Jamaica's economic turnaround, even if the US persons had given their support, without the support of the financially weak public sector workers, the deal could not go forward. Secondly, the juxtaposition reveals how weak the sovereign government of a developing state is without a network of support, and while Jamaica should seek to overcome the factors which make it vulnerable and dependent, it should not consider that not needing to rely on its citizens is a sign of strength.

Hutton and Johnson (2017), and Thompson (2019a) agree that how a leader behaves is a function of how a leader is, and therefore personal qualities inform leadership qualities. Thompson, Prescod, and Montgomery (2020) suggest that to understand a political leader's policy preferences one needs to examine their political ideologies. Against this background, how Phillips approached the challenge he faced in seeking to rescue the Jamaican economy, is understand from his upbringing as well as his personal and political leadership philosophy and political ideologies. The first segment of the interview explores those issues.

The critical lessons from the Jamaican experience, as told by Phillips, are found in the sections "Confronting Major Challenges" through to "Tough Conditionalities". Phillips's rendition of how he engaged qualities of reimaginative leadership as he interprets them is found in the last section of the interview.

INTERVIEW WITH DR PETER PHILLIPS

Introduction

Childhood, Personal and Political Philosophy

Dr Canute Thompson (CT): Dr Phillips, could you please briefly describe your childhood upbringing, your education and training, and your entry into public service and politics?

Dr Peter Phillips (PP): I am a child of teachers. My father has a career culminating as a professor at The University of the West Indies. Apart from him, three of my four grandparents were teachers, and my mother was a civil servant. I was born when my father was a lecturer at Mico so Mico Teachers' College as it was called then is my earliest memory. I would say also if you talk about a concept – Manchester and independent small farming and aspiring Jamaican people is the other defining context. It is also significant because Manchester is a parish that has a very distinct history. It never had sugar, and this is an analysis that in a sense came after realizing some of the values. It never had sugar such as it had slavery like everywhere else in Jamaica, but it had often smaller units organized around cattle and coffee, and it became the typical form in which most small farmers operated virtue of the topography. Post-1838 a lot of small farmers, independent people who had either been on plantation or bought property or had saved up in the interstice season of slavery managed to establish themselves and so you had at the heart of it this independent aspiring farmer commercial community that became the foundation in many respects of our striving for nationhood. Obviously, it wasn't all Manchester but by the same token I do not think it was an accident that Thomas Manley, Norman Manley's father was a Manchester man also growing oranges, trying to trade and all of that. My great-grand developed the ortanique and was a kind of adventurer in terms of entrepreneurial adventurer, was a Justice of the Peace during the earlier times. He did things like travelling to see if he could establish silk farms in Jamaica and with mulberry bushes to be imported from China. My great-granduncle B. B. Phillips sent his children away to Harvard University in the second and third decade of the twentieth century. There was that kind of impulse that I think would have helped shape me. My own grandfather would have gone to Panama, return, gone to Cuba and establish them essentially as a small farmer and my father's siblings did the route of Mico and farm school. So, there is this strong sense of independence, strong commitment to nationhood which was very much developed.

CT: You have partially addressed my second and third questions, namely:
- How did your childhood experiences, your education and training and your early political life and public service shape your political ideology?
- Could you describe the key tenets of your political ideology?

You have mentioned that that ideology has been shaped by a strong sense of independence and strong sense of nationhood.

PP: My father who shared room with Howard Cooke at Mico and they shared room again in London and later at Hans Crescent but that grouping of the Phillips, Howard Cooke, Reg. Murray and others were scenes of nation building – a notion coming off the PNP. The PNP was formed on the basis that this great nation building project was the culmination of that which previous generations had been looking [for].

My father had a strong sense that if your country has educated you, you need to devote that education back to the society. A strong sense of collective responsibility as the counterpoint to the heavy individualism which dominates today – that all great achievements are collective achievements. Those would have been the building blocks I think of the kind of early eon-structured social political philosophy.

Then later on coming out of high school, I went to Jamaica College and having done two years my father was in Britain, added to that a sense of African identity, black power ideology, pan-African identity which emerged and I think in hindsight partly out of an encounter with a lot of racist Britain because Britain was decolonizing and where I went to, did one year of primary school and one year at grammar school, but you were facing a lot of these returning colonialists coming out of Kenya. This really helped, predisposed in the late '60s to an interest in black liberation, ideologies and relative, students in the states who were sending things about Stokely Carmichael, Ralph Brown, Elijah, Malcolm X.

I had, in the Jamaican expression of it, come through Rastafari for a time and Walter Rodney who we were close to and were involved in the lecture series that he was carrying out. A group of us out of Jamaica College and some others were a part of the student protest of 1968 protesting Rodney's exclusion from the country.

Thus the principle of equality was strongly embedded in my consciousness, which has a strand going back into socialism as a strand of thought linking to decolonization and the basic claim of quality of states and of all people which the decolonization of the African world and the Asian world would have expressed a notion of individual rights but embedded in the collective responsibility of society to provide quality of opportunity to be particularly caring for the most vulnerable in society. Those are the main tenets. There are some books on liberation and education which my father would place in my room, and just said he thinks I would find them helpful. I guess I grew up in a family with two or three generations going back who saw education as the route, the vehicle of progress.

CT: If I may summarize Dr Phillips, you came out of family that had a strong teaching background located in parts of rural Jamaica not confined however by the post-slavery restrictions. You were able to pursue education as a vehicle of personal development but there was a family philosophy, an ideology, if you will, that understood that personal achievement was to be in the support systems of communities and country and such progress as an individual would have made, must be understood as being a gift from one's community and country.

PP: Absolutely, my father when I was ten or eleven years, would put me in the car and drive through Jones Town and Trench Town, Four Shore Road as it was called then, he said the country can't remain like this without preaching. He was an academic also not preaching but just exposing you as a middle-class child of a university professor or university senior lecturer, there is this world and changing this world was your obligation. My father was a democrat. I realize from his reading habits because there wasn't a lot of preaching but a lot of exposure to the literature of Ralph Ellison, James Baldwin, black American literature Claude McKay that was around in the house for you to read. The first person who gave me a communist manifesto was a staunch democrat. My father just gave it to me without commenting you might want to read this. He was going through UWI bookshop saw it and figured his son might want to read it. By this time, I was boarding at JC, he just brought it and gave it to me to read. I had an environment of explorational ideas often carry them to an extreme which he didn't agree with later but nevertheless it was a home environment which validated free thinking.

CT: So, you are saying that the key elements of the political ideology that you formulated, and which later embodied how you approached political service, emphasized equality.

PP: The fundamental equality of the human being for a world shaped by racism, by class, oppression that was very extreme and which today our people haven't even escaped from our culture today still bears the imprint of that racism. When you see young people trying to bleach their skin today 2020 you realize how pernicious and how enduring these cultural structures of derogation of a whole race is, and the persistence of the mountain of social inequality. But in our case, it is linked with all kinds of badges of oppression and classism.

Opportunity to Apply Ideological Beliefs
Entry to the Cabinet

CT: Your argument is that Jamaica has historically faced issues of racism and oppression, and that these issues somehow have distorted our social identity. You are further contending that these issues are present today and have been part of the narrative of our collective experience.

You became finance minister at a crucial time of Jamaica's political and economic life, which would have as a backdrop the issues of racism and oppression which you say are still part of our collective experience. But your service as a cabinet minister goes back to the 1990s. How did you seek to address, from the role of your cabinet position, the major issues which shaped the collective experience of Jamaicans?

PP: In the 1990s I was minister at Jamaica House. Minister of Special Projects in the Office of the Prime Minister and then Minister of Health and the Minister of Transport and Works and then Minister of National Security.

The Year 2012
Critical Issues Facing Jamaica

CT: So, in 2012 you would have come to that particular task with that body of experience rooted not only in your upbringing which would have shaped some philosophical ideas in a kind of broad melting pot, which drew on both African and Asian and the roots of the family, but a ministerial track record and experience. Given what you understood as the key issues facing Jamaica at the time you became minister of finance, how did you interpret your role and responsibilities and the critical priorities which faced the country?

PP: In 2012 the overarching challenge that faced Jamaica was the survival of the country. The issue with which the government had to wrestle was how to prevent total dislocation of Jamaican society which results from the disappearance of our reserves and closure of external sources of financing from global financial markets and from international agencies.

That was the most striking feature, and it is like being in a maze, there is only one gate that is visible at the time and the gate was really an affront programme. Only one gate available so how to pass through that gate was the main challenge. It is hard for people to understand when a driver skillfully avoids a crash it is not the same thing as surviving a crash. As you watched the standard measure is that you would have to have three months of reserve in place. As we watched our reserves come down to eight weeks, seven weeks, six weeks our reserves having to use it up and we are being, in a sense, run around the mulberry bush so to speak by the funding agencies; it got to a very extreme situation.

CT: With survival being the number one priority how did you set about identifying the key actions that needed to be taken to secure that survival and could you elaborate on the elements of survival? What would that survival mean? You mentioned about the question of reserves – what were the other critical elements of survival and how did you go about it?

PP: If reserves had disappeared it would have meant that our productive sector and our financial sector would have lost all their lines of credit, all of the normal financial arrangement which would herald things like major shortages for essentials, pharmaceutical, foodstuff because firms in a country that had no reserves no fund programme would have lost their lines of credit. The normal line of trade credit and that in turn would have meant a lot of political pressure and social disorder that would have resulted should that have taken place.

CT: This would also have had implications for paying public sector workers.

PP: It would have had implications. The first pressure of all would have been balance of payment problems.

CT: Meaning what?

PP: Meaning that you do not have enough money to pay for what you need to survive. You are a country that in effect imports. Your trade imports and exports represent 70 and 80 per cent of the total small open island economy, that to have foreign exchange when you don't have enough and the failure to have it would impair all your productive activities paying for basic supplies.

Placing the Challenges in Historical Context
Whither Jamaica's Vulnerability

CT: So our inherited vulnerability as a small island state was exacerbated by a number of developments?

PP: It may be semantic, but I would not call smallness a vulnerability. The world has big and small land masses, there are small islands which are successful and some which are not. I think though that that is a feature of much of our economic literature, but I do not agree with that position.

CT: Our vulnerability you are arguing is not necessarily a function of our size. It is a function of other things.

PP: Most, if not all, is result from poor management of our situation.

CT: So, it is a kind of created vulnerability.

PP: Vulnerability may have been exacerbated by historical factors. Countries develop agriculture primarily to feed themselves, we develop it because of history to feed others and that it created a certain pressure on your balance of payment. I remember Arthur Brown in a conversation saying that until we deal with the problem of food security as a country, we will always have pressure on our balance of payment because most places don't begin to spend a major share of their earnings to feed an imported taste. The staples are usually things that you grow, our staples are things we import. That is another whole space of economic history.

Top Priorities
Confronting the Major Challenges

CT: What would you say was the key priority you identified in leading the response to this state of imperative to survive?

PP: First of all, keep the country functioning. Secondly, immediately embark upon the discussions with the IMF which would be in the first week of assuming office to start the discussion. That would have meant those discussions ultimately leading to a programme which would have unlocked access to foreign exchange resources, many of which were committed but which we could not draw down in the absence of a programme - European Union, IDB. Apart from Venezuela with the oil facility which was a blessing and China which was doing work, all other funds were tied to getting the IMF seal of approval.

CT: You mentioned earlier being run around the mulberry bush by funding agencies as you sought to pursue this mandate to survive. In doing the things necessary to moving the country from this very precarious position you faced I assume challenges, resistance, opposition both internally within these parameters of the government probably as well as maybe from forces within the country more broadly. Could you talk about some of the challenges you faced whether internally or externally in pursuing the priorities that you saw necessary and how you met those challenges?

PP: I don't think there was any insurmountable challenge domestically. There were the usual kinds of political issues on the domestic front, but it is usually easier to deal with those when government just assumes office.

Overcoming Political Tribalism

There were people, for example, who would have wanted to change the leadership of some of the institutions, the BOJ for example. Bryan Wynter had replaced the former governor Lattibeaudiere during the Golding / Holness administration and in the usual kind of excesses of what you would call tribalist politics and our excessively divisive political culture, some wanted me to reinstate Lattibeaudiere. But that was more or less easily resisted.

I took the view that as much stability as was possible was desirable and that the country did not need any lurches or more potential for dislocation. We needed the people who had been involved in the thing because by and large I believe we are well served by a team of technically competent independent public servants. There was the need to assess the competence of who we had in place and there was a need also to begin a discussion with the key stakeholders locally, primarily financial institutions, trade unions etc.

Trust Deficit
Obstacles to Re-Starting Discussions with the IMF

CT: One of the greatest obstacles you faced was getting the derailed IMF Agreement (which was inherited from the previous government), back on track. Could you talk about the process, the personal pain (if any), and the problems you encountered and the point at which you began to see progress?

PP: The centrepiece of the effort was restarting the discussions with international agencies. There was a programme that had gone off the rails. There was a huge trust deficit and there was a need to try to engage and define the parameters of a new programme. The Fund sent an Article IV review team down here in the first two weeks and that defined what we needed to do. They set some basic parameters for the first budget which would have been the 2012–2013 budget which was aimed at getting the primary surplus back on target. It was a higher target than the previous administration had had because they had failed.

We were going awry and the country, despite the debt exchange, was not able to meet its obligations under the JDX certificate so that happened. Ultimately, as the situation became (about October 2012) quite urgent – the reserves were falling, and they are not releasing money even though you think your discussions are going reasonably well. As it turned out, although it took us a time to figure it out the major current of thought within the Fund was "let Jamaica crash" and we concentrated the mind and built an awareness of the need to fulfill the programme requirements and that's the result directly of trust deficit that existed.

CT: You are confirming that the report in the Financial Times and other media in 2012 which suggest that the unofficial/official position of the international financial community that the best position was to let Jamaica crash, was indeed true? How did those perceptions affect you in your negotiations and how did you navigate them?

PP: It is the first confirmation independently of what it took us a time to determine but I give you one of the clearest signals. We thought we were making progress and it turned out that at the Tokyo meetings of the World Bank and the IMF, I made a direct representation to the deputy managing director of the Fund who had oversight responsibility for Jamaica to unlock resources committed by the IDB, but which they would not allow us to draw down in the absence of the Fund agreeing to the draw-down. All that was needed was a simple letter from the Fund that would have said our discussions have proceeded far so we have no objection paying over these funds.

Sobering Refusal and Direct Insult

Their refusal was sobering for two reasons: (1) it showed that our judgement of good faith progress was not shared by the Fund; but (2) the way the decision was communicated carried a quality of direct insult to the country. This was both painful and angering. Simply put, I had a discussion with this fellow and he heard me and certainly he would let me know the answer shortly by the following day or the day after and then when I made my enquiry about the answer I discovered that he had left Tokyo and gone to some other part of Asia and sent some junior officer to tell me as Minister of Finance of Jamaica that the answer was no.

So, it not only carried the negative that was disturbing but the way it was done. This is part of the indignities as I mentioned in the parliament, and I think a series of what people had to face which is one of the reasons I said we had to ensure that we never get there again.

Broader Strategy: Build Other Alliances

So, what we had to do at that point is pursue a broader strategy that just didn't involve what was a political decision that was being faced. We needed to mobilize resources more widely, so we sought to make a direct outreach to the US authorities to make the simple point that they had to pay attention to the difficulties which Jamaica faced. In simple terms, if Jamaica crashed, Jamaican citizens would not be heading to Tokyo and China in droves, they would be heading to South Florida and New York.

The language was a bit colourful but I had to try to concentrate their minds on the enormity of the challenge we faced. Our strategy included reaching out to the Congressional Black Caucus as well as people in the US administration who were sympathetic to Jamaica. You have some Americans, connected Americans, wealthy Americans with villas in the North Coast that we contacted and tried to get them to get a word to senior officials of the Obama administration who could fix things.

CT: Let me put the pieces together. There was an underlying trust deficit. There would have been previous attempts at economic reform, previous initiatives going back to the previous administration. There would have been other attempts at drastic economic reforms such as the Jamaica Debt Exchange and the National Debt Exchange, but despite these efforts, Jamaica was in a quandary. In those circumstances, how do you as Minister of Finance move the country forward?

The Agreement
Tough Conditionalities

PP: Convince them of our goodwill, of our sincerity, of our commitment to doing it and to find a reasonable programme

CT: So, part of the trust deficit had to do with the funders' apprehension about Jamaica's good intent. Even before we came to what the content of that programme would have been there was that doubt about whether we were committed to it so that was the first hurdle you had to overcome?

PP: It is hard to overcome it because oftentimes it is unspoken.

CT: You get cues but nothing explicit?

PP: Cues and unreasonable provisions are insisted upon and your resistance which is based on technical grounds and do-ability practically is often thought to be a resistance borne of the fact that you do not want to do anything at all so the discussion is not really being sincere.

CT: So the point you made earlier where you said that there was this unofficial position "let Jamaica crash" about which the Financial Times reported earlier and a subsequent comment by the then head of the IMF about Jamaica being a pariah state all of those characterize the kind of environment within which you operated. What did you pursue (in the negotiations) as the key pillars of a transformed Jamaican economy and how would you assess what was secured?

PP: Politically you had people who were saying to us the then opposition "sign, sign anything", almost saying sign now as the apprehension goes there is the pressure that just accept anything. It would have been the worst thing because if you just sign something that was undoable you would have just deepened the mistrust.

CT: So, you endured the kind of pushback and disrespect how would you describe your navigating of that level of mistrust and apprehension?

PP: I think in part fortune smiled on us and in part our own effort. Fortune smiled on us because there was a change in leadership in the western hemisphere division of the fund.

This would probably have been around September-October – the latter part of the year. Which meant that you had someone who was not prisoner of the previous experience who was not a Fund member at all. He came from outside of the Fund. The director of the western hemisphere still had the handle. I remember meeting him in Panama City where the IDB had meetings and for the first time it became clear that here was somebody who wasn't carrying belly for Jamaica who would deal with it so you could get a clear sense of what were the fundamental parameters of a programme, what it would look like. As I said the high point otherwise was December by that time we had to prepare for the 2013–2014 budget. They basically said the new financial secretary Devon Rowe and the governor of the Bank of Jamaica had to go to Washington and stayed there until we got a programme. So, they spent time there and they came back Christmas eve, went back up right after new year and stayed and hammered out the basic contours.

CT: Tell us about the basic contours of that agreement.

PP: A pretty heavy primary surplus target (7.5 per cent) at the time. It involved a wage freeze; it involved another debt exchange and there were other elements in the budget that we insisted upon and which we got. There should have been a floor for social expenditure and there were other things, the removal of customs waiver systems and all of that, tax on provisions, tax refund. Most importantly were the preconditions that were set – there was major taxation, get the unions to sign unto a wage freeze and get the debt exchange.

CT: How fundamentally different was this agreement from the previous agreements?

PP: Higher primary surplus. It was up by 1.5 per cent of GDP over the previous 6 per cent, which was hardly met. We were 4 and 4.5 per cent. At 7.5 per cent this was a steeper hill to climb.

But even after 7.5 per cent was agreed in principle the Fund was reluctant to give us the programme because the longest period was a 3-year programme which they could not bring the debt down to 100 per cent of GDP.

CT: So, the key elements of the programmes were higher primary surplus, one of the highest in the world, major taxation, and wage freeze.

The economic turnaround required great sacrifice on the part of Jamaicans – taxpayers, public sector workers, all others. How would you characterize the sacrifices that the public made how would you describe the response the public made to this programme?

PP: It was good, difficult but good. We had to convince the public, all the stakeholders particularly the banks and the trade unions. I could understand the situation with the banks because they had just done a JDX before which involved their giving up permits and found that they had given it up, but they still were being asked to make further sacrifice without government having fulfilled its responsibility from the first debt exchange. But all of that was in the discussion that led to EPOC. We were prepared to be totally open to everything. This is a sign that there was nothing under the table. We opened the entirety of the government accounts to you through EPOC and we would report regularly, once per month and you are free to report to the public without interference.

CT: So EPOC was the mechanism used to build trust. In wrapping up I would like to ask two questions. I would like to go to question fifteen. I have argued that effective sustainable leadership requires several fundamentals some of which are listed here and some of which my research has unearthed. Could you talk a little bit about these qualities and the extent to which on reflection any of these might have informed how you approach your work and whether they form part of your overall driving philosophy and how you led this transformation?

Leadership Philosophy
Whither Elements of Reimaginative Leadership

CT: In my theory of reimaginative leadership I identify nine qualities of the leader who exercises the skill of reimagination. These qualities are:

i. The capacity for alternatives-thinking
ii. People empowerment
iii. The reliance on influence rather than power to produce results
iv. Mutual accountability
v. The capacity to influence change
vi. The exercise of courage despite clear 'danger'
vii. The demonstration of care
viii. The commitment to justice (which includes showing deference to the opinions and capacities of others, as against excluding them)
ix. The building and maintaining of trustful relationships.

PP: I was struck by this, and I certainly think it summarizes my own thinking, but I would probably express some of the ideas slightly differently. First, I think good leadership is rooted in sincerity of purpose. You must develop some basic principles, you must be honest, straightforward, being objective. This does not mean you are naïve. You can't go and announce your tax package early for people to take advantage of it – it is just common sense, reservations but you need to be open about choices that you face you need to be willing to discuss alternatives and carry people through. If you have a position don't be too pig-headed that you are unwilling to adjust if a better view is presented. If the people are not persuaded use reason not power to get them to see the option, you are offering. I am an absolute believer in what Michael Manley calls the politics of participation or what I call the politics of consultation. There is no wisdom that is automatically in a minister or ministry because they are charged officially with policy making. Good wisdom is all around. The book of Proverbs says wisdom cries out in the street and no one hears. Your duty is to go to the street and embrace wisdom and I think transparency which is linked to the sincerity. Absolutely important proposition and of course always must remember the ultimate philosophical ideological diction of social justice that must not only be done but seem to be done.

CT: What does social justice mean?

PP: It means for example it is widely insisted that the programme had to have a floor below which social expenditure could not fall. You couldn't ask the poorest to make a sacrifice which would carry them further into destitution. We have an objective to correct the historical wrongs that have left too many without the ability to enjoy the basic possibilities of life of their times. Education, basic health care and to enjoy the fruits of civilization. I think every society has an obligation to all its people in that way. That is a separate meaning of development. We believe in the equality of the human being every man is endowed with a basic humanity which demands dignity in their treatment. Simultaneously that factor of humanity means that you ought not to be subjected to oppressive, demeaning, undignified circumstances and that despite the obvious fact that people are endowed with different talents and gifts there is a certain basic quality of existence that humanity demands and it is the obligation of society and all states to ensure that that is there and that ideally in every state you have the opportunity to rise to the fullest extent that your own efforts and talents are not to be denied by virtue of the prejudices of class or race or oppressive structures of our society.

CT: Thank you very much Dr. Phillips.

CHAPTER 12
Conclusion: Reimaginative Leadership Pre-21st Century and in the 21st Century

Reimaginative leadership, as has been shown in the discussion on the philosophical roots of the construct, is not a twenty-first century phenomenon. There have been shining examples throughout history of this kind of leadership. This final chapter exploresexamples of reimaginative leadership as expressed in the public life of international personalities. Some of these personalities are well known twentieth-century figures but those from earlier periods may not be as well known. Six individuals are discussed in this chapter and their selection was based largely on the extent to which they displayed the reimaginative leadership qualities of courage, manifested in constructive subversion, as well as alternatives-thinking. Other personalities could, no doubt be selected.

Rosa Parks

Rosa Parks (1913–2005) may be described as the matriarch of the civil rights movement in the United States of America. The protest movement against racial segregation and mistreatment of Black people, perhaps received its biggest boost on 1 December 1955 when she refused to give up her seat, on the instructions of the bus driver, to a white passenger.

Parks, a resident of the state of Alabama, was returning home from work on that day on which she was catapulted into the annals of history. Public buses had sections reserved for White passengers at the front of the buses. A moveable sign would indicate where the dividing line was, however if the number of White passengers exceeded the number of seats designated for them, the bus driver had the authority to instruct Blacks to vacate their seats and give same to White passengers, having shifted the sign towards the back.

On the day in question, Parks was instructed to vacate her seat so that a White person could have it. She refused and was arrested in keeping with the prevailing laws. Notwithstanding her relase on bail that same night, the National Association for the Advancement of Colored People (NAACP) began to mobilize its membership for mass protests. In the days that followed, many buses ran virtually empty and the city's revenues were severely cut as a result of the protest.

Parks is often quoted as saying that her feet were tired and that she was not getting up, but in later years she clarified that she was not too physically tired to get up but she was tired of giving up and that is why she refused to get up. Parks' defiance led to nationwide efforts to end racial segregation of public facilities. Parks' defiance, though partly a function of tiredness, was, more importantly, a demonstration of an understanding of the issues that confronted not only her but the community of Blacks. In the face of White oppression, (and indeed any form of oppression) the appropriate response could not be submission and compliance, if one is to exercise agency and personal sovereignty. The response must be resistance. Resistance requires courage. This is exactly what Parks did and showed, and her action sparked a wave of protest which redefined the course of American history.

John Wyclif

John Wyclif lived in the fourteenth century. He was a member of the Catholic church but history records that Wyclif was no friend of the Catholic hierarchy. He was known for calling into question notions of papal infallibility and declaring that a worldly pope was a heretic and should be removed. Contrary to accepted doctrine, Wyclif taught that the true church was "invisible", made up of only the elect of God and that no visible church or its officers can control entrance or exclude membership. This position he took in response to the chief weapon of punishment used by the church against dissenting members, namely excommunication.

Against the will of Catholic leadership, Wyclif translated the Bible into English from the Latin vulgate. He insisted that scripture held the supreme authority in life and that even the unlettered could understand it. This view that ordinary people could understand scripture was like oil on flames for the Catholic church leadership which held that the pope was the final and binding authority in the interpretation of scripture and that apart from the pope only trained priests had the authority to interpret scripture. Needless to say, the Catholic church despised Wyclif. In 1415, the council of Constance condemned Wyclif and ordered his writings to be burned. They also ordered that the bones of Wyclif, (who died in 1384) be exhumed and cast out of the consecrated ground where he was buried and in 1428, under papal command, his remains were dug up, burned, and the ashes were thrown in a nearby stream on the basis that his reckless disobedience of holy ordinances rendered him unworthy to have a place in the consecrated and sacred burial place.

Jan Hus

Jan Hus is the father of the Moravian movement, now named the Moravian church or Unity of the Brethren. Hus, who lived from 1369–1415, became the chief exponent and defender of Wyclif at Prague University where he was appointed dean of the faculty of philosophy in 1402. Drawing large crowds, he became an extremely popular preacher among the common people and the aristocracy. Hus sought to reach the general populace with the word of God by preaching in Czech as well as Latin.

Hus's themes were staunchly anti-clergy. His reputation for unblemished purity stood in sharp contrast with the corruption and worldliness of the existing religious clergy, especially in Bohemia. He denounced evil and immorality in the church. He once wrote, "The church shines in its walls, but starves in its poor saints; it clothes its stones with gold, but leaves its children naked". He, like Wyclif, held that popes were not inerrant but some had been heretics! Hus is sometimes referred to as the forerunner of the Protestant reformation. Martin Luther, champion of the reformation, credits Hus as the main source of his inspiration. Hus's unrelenting challenge to the leadership of the church was the basis on which the church decided to silence him. In 1415 he was burnt at the stake. When his dying body fell to the ground, his heart still beating, the church leaders who had gathered to see his ignominious death, began to beat his moving heart to ensure his complete death. Such hostility by leaders to those who oppose them would undoubtedly spark both fear and resentment. While leaders of today's church may not use that form of punishment to silence critics some of the means used are nonetheless exceedingly cruel and when these become known to members and would-be members many lose respect for and confidence in the leadership of the church.

Karl Barth

Karl Barth was one of the most influential theologians of the twentieth century. A German scholar (1886–1968), the totality of his works exceeded six million words, captured mainly in his thirty-one-volume publication on theology. Barth's theology remains required or recommended reading across many theological schools.

Barth's influence was not so much his theological treatise but his public engagement in which he established a link between theology and ethics. Ethics, he argued, framed the relationship among human beings, and was a tool for interpreting and addressing the vexing problems that faced human society. In defining his approach to the practice of ethics, Barth held the Bible in one hand and the newspaper in the other.

Barth's theology was shaped by his experience of living and teaching in Germany during the rise of Nazism and he stood as a moral voice challenging the society and the church to a higher way of leading and living. History notes that by 1934, Barth had become a leader in the confessing church movement, which stood in courageous opposition to Nazism at a time when the German protestant church had largely endorsed National Socialism. This stance cost him his professorship at Bonn University, and he was forced to flee the country in 1935.

Martin Luther King, Jr.

Martin Luther King, Jr. was a leading, if not the leading civil rights advocate and clergyman of his time. He was born in 1929 to into a family of pastors. His grandfather and his father served as pastors of the famed Ebeneezer Baptist Church in Atlanta. He was assassinated in 1968, at a time when he advocacy for change in race relations and justice for marginalized people, particularly African-American, was gaining momentum. King had a vision of an American society in which opportunity was available to all regardless of skin colour.

Although many of the battles King fought were described as *civil rights* advocacy, and involved the federal and various state governments of the United States of America, he too was involved in very intense fights (in some instances secret and subtle) with the leadership of the church. King's fight with the leadership of the church, not just the Baptist denomination, epitomized the concept of an enemy within, as thus the challenge of successfully pursuing an agenda when key stakeholders are not on board. The nature of this struggle in outlined in King's famous April 18, 1963, letter from Birmingham Jail. The letter was written in response to a statement published in a local newspaper by leading church leaders criticising King's civil rights advocacy approach and urging him to seek to have his issues resolved through the courts.

The statement by the senior leadership of eight denominations (Christian and Muslim) was written while he was incarcerated in Alabama (on charges of provoking civil disobedience) and urged him to cease from his path of demanding equal rights for Blacks and let the courts deal with those matters. The basic argument of the church leaders was that the kind of agenda that King (as a clergyman) was pursuing was inconsistent with the mission, style and purpose of the church, and his actions were having an adverse impact on the reputation of the church and people of faith.

In his response, King expressed surprise and disappointment at the position of the leaders who expressed concern about the demonstrations (that King's movement had ostensibly sparked) but not the conditions that had brought those demonstrations about. King also blasted the seeming hope and confidence of these clergymen in the judicial system, given that they had urged him to **wait** and allow the process to take its course. King's dismissal of their position was based on the fact that Africans and Afro-Americans and other peoples of African descent had been waiting for centuries to be given a fair hearing.

It is a profound lesson of history that few people, if asked, could name any of the eight clergymen who signed that letter to which King was responding. One of the key characteristics these clergymen shared, which contrasted with King's, was their commitment to preserving, or at least not challenging, the status quo. King, on the other hand, was not unwilling to challenge the status quo. For their faithfulness to the status quo, these clergymen are virtually forgotten in the annals of history. For his diligent and courageous assault on the status quo King has been immortalized, even though assassinated at a fairly young age.

The interplay of the fortunes of those who protect and defend the status quo, versus the fortunes of those who are willing to undertake the *reimaginative critique* of the status quo is also seen in the narrative of King's engagement with the political establishment. A key historical figure in the attempts to place a lid on the advocacy efforts of King, was the police chief of Alabama. His task was to use all means (legal and illegal, and of course even lethal) to bring King to book. These included attack dogs being loosed on peaceful demonstrators, children being rounded up and placed on trucks and taken to prison, and probably even assassination. Again, for his staunch defence of the status quo, and no doubt his honourable discharge and retirement, history has forgotten the Alabama police chief of the day, one Mr Connors. King on the other hand is immortalized.

The stories of Wyclif, Hus and King have a few key characteristics in common. Chief of these are (a) that the leaders whose actions they called into question and the systems (status quos) whose modus operandi they questioned were not prepared to yield without a fight. But, the breaking point came nonetheless, even though all three died or were killed before the goals for which they fought were realized; and (b) that history has found an enduring place for them while it has forgotten those who opposed them.

The lessons inherent in this are simple. The reimaginative leader must be willing to persevere; must be willing to put in a big sacrifice – even that of their own life; and must be clear on the agenda they are pursuing and continuously articulate and advocate that agenda.

Nelson Mandela

Nelson Mandela who was the first Black President of South Africa was born in 1918. He served as President from 1994 to 1999. His rise to the presidency occurred three years after his release from prison in 1991, where he was serving a life sentence for treason. His release in 1991 was after he had served twenty-seven years in jail. Despite his nearly three decades of incarceration, he continued to serve as leader of the political party the African National Congress (ANC).

South Africa was the bastion of White racism which practiced the apartheid system. The system was introduced in 1948 under the White nationalist party. Under this system, whites were seen as superior to Blacks. The social, education, and economic system was based on separation of Blacks from Whites, and the latter lived in splendour while the former lived, for the most part in squalor.

A central pillar of the apartheid system was that the church, particularly the Dutch reformed church, played an important role in promoting the system as consistent with the teachings of scripture. Mandela's lifetime fight was against the system of apartheid. Having led the fight, he was charged and found guilty of treason – which carried the death penalty.

Mandela was, however, given a sentence of life imprisonment.

One of the most significant parts of the story of Mandela is that he could have spared himself twenty-seven years in prison by simply giving the leaders of South Africa a commitment that he would accept being muzzled and in effect abandon the cause of the African National Congress. He could have avoided the pain of isolation in the Robben Island jail. But as a reimaginative leader, he understood that he was answerable not only to himself and that the value of his life was to be found not in what he got but in what he gave. As such, he was prepared for the big sacrifice and counted his life as nothing while he pursued his cause. His selfless sacrifice earned him many accolades, including the Nobel Peace Prize. The larger accolades he received include the undying respect of the majority of the world's citizens. His captors who led the nation of South Africa, and who received the endorsement of the Dutch reformed church, have been decimated in the pages of history and assigned the roles of the scorned counterfoils.

One of the questions that the nation of South Africa will be forced to asked, however, is whether the changes to the socio-economic arrangements in that country post-apartheid have gone far enough and whether Mandela, specifically, had done enough to ensure that the economic disadvantages suffered by Blacks were not perpetuated. Despite the shortcomings that his presidency may show in this regard, the mission of his life was to overthrow the system of apartheid politically. The mission of his successors is to correct the structural economic imbalances.

Mia Mottley – Prime Minister of Barbados

Mia Mottley has been Prime Minister of the Caribbean Island of Barbados since 2018. Mottley has emerged on the global stage as a world leader based on her capacity to clearly articulate the nature of issues the Caribbean region and the world is confronting (on issues such as climate change, debt, carbon emissions, inequity, and disenfranchisement of sectors of society. She has demonstrated many of the qualities of the reimaginative leader, particularly alternatives-thinking (which is a solutions-finding mode of leading) and courage to call others to account, reflecting the ethic of mutual accountability.

In her speech at the 2021 UN General Assembly, she abandoned her prepared text and held an expansive and informal conversation with world leaders as she mused on some deep issues facing the world. She urged world leaders to use their influence (which she described as "the power of the pen") to amend debt arrangements between global financial institutions and developing countries, wherein they would impose natural disaster and pandemic clauses in developing countries' debt. She also called for the removal of barriers to accessing financial assistance from multilateral development banks.

Reimaginative leadership is also 'disruptive' – To be disturbing and unsettling the status quo, making "trouble" and persisting in pursuing a path that is contrary to others' comfort zones. Mottley's bold speech in November 2021, made to the banking sector in Barbados in challenged banks to get out of the business of being merely security firms for people's money and charging them a fee and get back to the business of intervention by using the resources of depositors for advancing the wealth of the many. She also challenged the banks to consider and revisit the rates they paid on deposits versus what they charged on loans and credit cards and called for a review of fee income policy. Such a challenge coming from a Prime Minister represented a radical and courageous departure from how Prime Ministers customarily address the money sectors of their societies.

Mottley's well-watched speech at the Climate Conference in Glasgow in October 2021 was also disruptive. It that speech she highlighted the fact that in the preceding thirteen years, Central Banks of the world's richest countries engaged in $25 trillion of quantitative easing, $9 trillion of which was in the preceding eighteen months (the COVID-19 era). Quantitative easing is strategy used by central banks to pump more money into economies to force the lowering of interest rates and thereby simulating economic activity. This strategy is used when there is an economic crisis and to halt the impact of that crisis, governments borrow, tap into reserves, and buy bonds and stocks to increase money flowing in the economy. This move helps businesses get back into operation early. Prime Minister Mottley's point was that in the same way rich countries could have engaged in quantitative easing in response to various global crises in the preceding thirteen years, with one-third of the funds in the last year and a half (COVID-19), they could have done similarly to address the global climate crisis.

The reimaginative acts of being discursive, inquisitive, incisive, disruptive, bold, and unsettling are not ends in themselves, they are means to ends and represent taking a stance for something. The positions taken by reimaginative leaders are intended to stimulate action towards a larger good, and they are prepared to do so at whatever political costs they incur.

Jacinda Ardern – New Zealand

Jacinda Ardern, born in 1980, served as the fortieth Prime Minister of New Zealand from 2017 to 2023, and was the world's youngest Head of State at the time she became prime minister. One of her greatest challenges as leader of the country was the management of the COVID-19 pandemic.

Scholars and public opinion leaders (Friedman 2020; Wilson 2020; Craig 2021; and Beattie and Priestly 2021), have hailed the leadership of Jacinda Ardern in her country's fight against, and the management of, the COVID-19 pandemic. Ardern has been praised as a model of qualities such as mutual accountability, trust-building, empathy, care, and a gracious listener. Her model of leadership during the pandemic has been seen as that of a skilled team leader leading a team of five million, (Beattie and Priestly 2021).

Friedman (2020) highlights Ardern's empathy and argues that her empathy was a major element in her effectiveness in leading New Zealand through the pandemic. Friedman suggests that Ardern's leadership style resonated with citizens of New Zealand

and thus produced the team-like atmosphere among the citizenry. This team-like spirit Wilson (2020) attributes to the shared sense of purpose which Ardern was able to successfully create. These analyses are further corroborated by Craig (2021), who discusses Ardern's qualities of kindness and courage, and states:,

> Jacinda Ardern's political success has in no small way been built upon a particular performative style that foregrounds communication skills across mass and social media, empathy and compassion, combined with firmness and constancy, and command of policy detail (289). (my emphasis).

The qualities of Ardern, as discussed above, are thoroughly consistent with the qualities of reimaginative leadership which have been described as firstly grounded in alternatives-thinking, thereby no stuck to traditional ways of doing things. Thus, the concepts of 'unsettled', 'disruptive' and 'explorative' which are central to the definition of leadership reimagination. Another central tenet of the paradigm of leadership reimagination, which was consistently and skilfully displayed by Ardern, are courage and change catalysation. Bromfield and McConnell (2021), discuss these qualities, and explore their role in the success that New Zealand (and Australia) had in fighting the COVID-19 pandemic.

APPENDIX 1: Qualities of Reimaginative Leadership

1. Is caring and compassionate
2. Pays attention to the concerns of others
3. Facilitates debate on issues related to the direction of the organization /department
4. Is open to exploring diverse approaches to solving problems that arise
5. Welcomes initiative
6. Sees mistakes as opportunities for improvement
7. Provides opportunities for others to lead
8. Welcomes criticisms of his/her points of view and opinions
9. Is not afraid to take an unpopular position
10. Negotiates even when under pressure
11. Consistently displays behaviours that reflect the core values of the organization
12. Inspires others to commit to the larger agenda
13. Helps others to see their role in the scheme of things
14. Delegates responsibilities to team members
15. Supports team members in the pursuit of their tasks
16. Is trustworthy
17. Holds himself accountable to those he/she leads
18. Celebrates the successes of team members
19. Places the organization above self
20. Provides regular updates on his/her performance

21. Provides team members with updates on their performance
22. Is willing to subject his/her ideas to debate before implementation
23. Is willing to allow others' ideas to replace his/her own based on outcomes of debate
24. Is ethical in his/her dealings
25. Embraces alternative ideas
26. Will implement ideas that originated with others
27. Is fair to others
28. Is willing to represent the concerns of others
29. Displays commitment in defending others who are treated unfairly
30. Does not blindly support the positions of the organization
31. Will challenge the organization if he/she thinks the organization is acting unwisely
32. Is balanced in his/her perspectives on issues that affect staff
33. Is balanced in his/her approach to the priorities of productivity and the needs of staff
34. Empowers others
35. Is a worthy representative of the organization
36. Helps staff understand the direction of the organization
37. Is a good listener
38. Enables others to improve their performance
39. Believes in others' abilities
40. Nurtures others' self-confidence
41. Pushes others beyond self-imposed limits
42. Does not try to dictate how people should see issues
43. Provides relevant information to staff
44. Respects the opinions of staff members
45. Respects the principles for which the organization stands

Appendix 1: Qualities of Reimaginative Leadership

46. Is a good role model
47. Inspires confidence in the work of the organization
48. Makes work an uplifting experience
49. Does not impose limits on others' potential
50. Gives challenging assignments
51. Gives opportunity for others to assume increased responsibilities
52. Does not assume that he/she always knows the right answer
53. Seeks the help of subordinates in finding solutions
54. Allows subordinates to participate in decision-making
55. Involves others in discussions on matters of high importance to the organization
56. Brings his/her values to bear on the organization
57. Offers candid criticisms most times
58. Is not afraid to pursue a path that is unpopular

APPENDIX 2: Survey Instrument

SA = Strongly Agree; A = Agree; U = Undecided; D = Disagree; SD = Strongly Disagree

	SA	A	U	D	SD
Do you think that in order to be an effective leader a principal should:					
1. Take an interest in the opinions of staff members					
2. Show high regard for the professional judgment of staff members					
3. Welcome the points of view of staff members even when those views are different to his/hers					
4. Respond positively even when there are disagreements between his/her views and that of staff members					
5. Resist any inclination on his or her part to dictate how staff members should think					
6. Show respect to staff members					
7. Make an effort to keep staff motivated					
8. Encourage staff members to continue to develop their professional skills					

Appendix 2: Survey Instrument

	SA	A	U	D	SD
Do you think that in order to be an effective leader a principal should:					
9. Demonstrate care for the needs of members of staff					
10. Seek to influence staff rather than use power to enforce his/her will					
11. Commend staff who demonstrate commitment					
12. Publicly recognize staff who produce spectacular results					
13. Admit error on his/her part when this is established					
14. Show a willingness to accept criticism					
15. Convey by his/her actions that views and approaches other than his/her own can be correct					
16. Show mastery of the job of school management					
17. Defer to other members of staff on matters on which they are more knowledgeable					
18. Model the behaviours he/she requires of staff members					
19. Be willing to debate issues on which there are diverse opinions					
20. Be willing to subject his/her positions to the collective wisdom of staff members					
21. Be a good listener					
22. Encourage diversity of perspectives					

	SA	A	U	D	SD
Do you think that in order to be an effective leader a principal should:					
23. Encourage camaraderie among staff members					
24. Promote collective responsibility					
25. Ensure performance evaluations are done of every staff member					
26. Ensure that low performing staff members receive support to improve					
27. Create the conditions for members of staff to participate in decision-making					
28. Lead in the development of a strategic plan					
29. Be trained in the fundamentals of strategic planning					
30. Be an advocate for justice					
31. Promote the value of learning from the successful practices of other schools					
32. Utilize the diverse strengths of members of staff in the operations of the school, in addition to their primary competencies					
33. Allow leaders to develop at all levels in the organization					
34. Be firm with repeated failures to meet standards of excellence					
35. Create an environment that makes work exciting					

Appendix 2: Survey Instrument   151

Please answer the following questions.

(1) Your age group is:
    (a) 20–30   [ ]
    (b) 31–40   [ ]
    (c) 41–50   [ ]
    (d) 51–60   [ ]
    (e) 60+   [ ]

(2) You have been a teacher for:
    (a) 5 years or less   [ ]
    (b) 6–10 years   [ ]
    (c) 11–15 years   [ ]
    (d) 16–20 years   [ ]
    (e) Over 20 years   [ ]

(3) You have been teaching at your current school for:
    (a) 5 years or less   [ ]
    (b) 6–10 years   [ ]
    (c) 11–15 years   [ ]
    (d) 16–20 years   [ ]
    (e) Over 20 years   [ ]

(4) Your highest professional qualification is:
    (a) Diploma   [ ]
    (b) Bachelor's Degree   [ ]
    (c) Master's Degree   [ ]
    (d) Postgraduate Cert in Education [ ]
    (e) Doctorate   [ ]

(5) You are:
    (a) Male   [ ]
    (b) Female   [ ]

(6) You currently teach at the:
   (a) Early Childhood Level   [ ]
   (b) Primary Level   [ ]
   (c) Secondary Level   [ ]
   (d) Tertiary Level   [ ]
   (e) Other _____   [ ]

(7) You are currently based in the:
   (a) Corporate area   [ ]
   (b) Rural area   [ ]

(8) You are currently working in a:
   (a) Public school   [ ]
   (b) Private school   [ ]

(9) You are a principal:
   (a) Yes   [ ]
   (b) No   [ ]

References

Alcoff, Linda Martin. 2019. Foreword in *Pedagogic of Liberation: A Latin American Philosophy of Education* by Enrique Dussel. Punctum Books.

Aliakbari, Mohammad, Elham Faraji, and Ilam University-Iran. 2011. "Basic Principles of Critical Pedagogy." *International Conference on Humanities, Historical and Social Sciences* 17 (January). https://www.researchgate.net/profile/Mohammad_Aliakbari/publication/266224451_Basic_Principles_of_Critical_Pedagogy/links/5488a7c40cf2ef344790a286.pdf.

Anthony, Scott D. 2014a. "Disruptive Trends to Watch in 2013." *Harvard Business Review*. August 7. https://hbr.org/2013/01/disruptive-trends-to-watch-in.

———. 2014b. "The Asian Innovation Century, Again." *Harvard Business Review*. August 7. https://hbr.org/2012/12/the-asian-innovation-century-a.

Asghar, Rob. 2014. "What Millennials Want In The Workplace (And Why You Should Start Giving It To Them)." *Forbes*, January 13. https://www.forbes.com/sites/robasghar/2014/01/13/what-millennials-want-in-the-workplace-and-why-you-should-start-giving-it-to-them/.

Bartsch, Vera, Mark Ebers, and Indre Maurer. 2013. "Learning in Project-Based Organizations: The Role of Project Teams' Social Capital for Overcoming Barriers to Learning." *International Journal of Project Management* 31 (2): 239–51. Elsevier BV. doi:10.1016/j.ijproman.2012.06.009.

Bass, Bernard. 1985. *Leadership and Performance*. New York: Free Press.

Beall, George. 2017. "8 Key Differences Between Gen Z and Millennials." *Huffpost*, November 6. https://www.huffpost.com/entry/8-key-differences-between_b_12814200.

Beattie, Alex, and Rebecca Priestley. 2021. "Fighting COVID-19 with the Team of 5 Million: Aotearoa New Zealand Government Communication during the 2020 Lockdown." *Social Sciences & Humanities Open* 4 (1): 100209. Elsevier BV. doi:10.1016/j.ssaho.2021.100209.

Beckett, Linnea, Ronald David Glass, and Ana Paulina Moreno. 2012. "A Pedagogy of Community Building: Re-Imagining Parent Involvement and Community Organizing in Popular Education Efforts." *Association of Mexican American Educators Journal* 6 (1): 5–14. https://amaejournal.utsa.edu/index.php/AMAE/article/download/97/88.

Bernstein, Jonathan. 2019. "Opinion | Has Trump Kept His Promises?" *The New York Times*, August 22. https://www.nytimes.com/2019/08/22/opinion/trump-promises-campaign-2016.html.

Biggs, Dick. 2005." Professional Development Communication." *http://biggspeaks.com/communication.html*.

Biography.com editors. "Rosa Parks Biography." https://www.biography.com/activist/rosa-parks

Bivins, Thomas. 2006. "Responsibility and Accountability." In *Ethics in Public Relations: Responsible Advocacy*, edited by Kathy Fitzpatrick and Carolyn Bronstein, 19–38. California: Sage.

Black, Jan Knippers. 2009.*The Politics of Human Rights Protection: Moving Intervention Upstream with Impact Assessment.* Lanham, MD: Rowman and Littlefield.

Blanchard, Ken. 2010. *Leading at a Higher Level*. New Jersey: Financial Times Press.

Blasé, Joseph, and Jo Blase. 1999. "Principals' Instructional Leadership and Teacher Development: Teachers' Perspectives." *Educational Administration Quarterly* 35 (3): 349–78. SAGE Publishing. doi:10.1177/0013161x99353003.

Boyden World Corporation. "Industry Insights: IBM Executives Lay Out New Growth Strategy." Accessed on June 11, 2019, https://www.boyden.com/media/ibm-executives-lay-out-new-growth-strategy-170192/index.html.

Bromfield, Nicholas, and Allan McConnell. 2020. "Two Routes to Precarious Success: Australia, New Zealand, COVID-19 and the Politics of Crisis Governance." *International Review of Administrative Sciences* 87 (3): 518–35. SAGE Publishing. doi:10.1177/0020852320972465.

Brueggemann, Walter. 1986. *David's Truth in Israel's Imagination and Memory*. Minneapolis, MN: Fortress Press.
———. 2018. *The Prophetic Imagination*. Minneapolis, MN: Fortress Press.
Burns, James. 1978. *Leadership*. New York: Harper and Row.
Burton, Brian K., and Craig P. Dunn. 1996. "Feminist Ethics as Moral Grounding for Stakeholder Theory." *Business Ethics Quarterly* 6 (2): 133–47. Philosophy Documentation Center. doi:10.2307/3857619.
Byham, William. 2012. *Taking Your Succession Management Plan into the 21st Century*. Bridgeville, PA: Development Dimensions International.
Cambridge Dictionary. "Meaning of Courage in English." Accessed June 11, 2019. https://dictionary.cambridge.org/dictionary/english/courage.
Carnegie, Dale. 2017. *How to Win Friends and Influence People*. London: Simon and Schuster.
Cavanaugh, William. 1998. *Torture and Eucharist: Theology, Politics and the Body of Christ*. Cambridge, MA: Blackwell.
Charles, Jacqueline. 2019. "Jamaica Once Couldn't Pay Its Light Bill. Now Its Economy Is Welcoming Porsche and BMW." *Miami Herald*, June 15. https://www.miamiherald.com/news/nation-world/world/americas/article231234653.html.
Chuang, Szufang. 2013. "Essential Skills for Leadership Effectiveness in Diverse Workplace Development." *Online Journal for Workforce Education and Development* 6 (1): 5. https://opensiuc.lib.siu.edu/cgi/viewcontent.cgi?article=1133&context=ojwed.
Clarke, Nigel. 2019. "Lessons from Jamaica for Small Countries with Big Debts." *Financial Times*, February 19. https://www.ft.com/content/04870fa8-2e12-11e9-80d2-7b637a9e1ba1.
Cohen, Michael. 2020. *Disloyal: A Memoir – The True Story of the Former Personal Attorney to President Donald J. Trump*. New York: Skyhorse Publishing.
Covey, Stephen R.. 1992. *Principle-centered Leadership*. New York: Free Press.
———. 2004. *The Seven Habits of Highly Effective People*. New York: Free Press.
Craig, Geoffrey. 2021. "Kindness and Control: The Political Leadership of Jacinda Ardern in the Aotearoa New Zealand

COVID-19 Media Conferences." *Journalism and Media* 2 (2): 288–304. Multidisciplinary Digital Publishing Institute. doi:10.3390/journalmedia2020017.

Darling-Hammond, Linda, Ruth Chung Wei, and Alethea Andree. 2010. "How High-Achieving Countries Develop Great Teachers. Research Brief." *Stanford Centre for Opportunity Policy in Education*, August. https://eric.ed.gov/?id=ED533011.

Damanpour, Fariborz. 1991. "Organizational Innovation: A Meta-analysis of Effects of Determinants and Moderators." *Academy of Management Journal* 34 (3): 555–90.

Dike, Victor E., Ken Odiwe and Donatus M. Ehujor. 2015. "Leadership and Management in the 21st Century Organizations: A Practical Approach." *World Journal of Social Science Research* 2 (2): 139–59. https://core.ac.uk/download/pdf/268085327.pdf.

Drucker, Peter. 1986. *The Effective Executive: The Definitive Guide to Getting the Right Things Done*. HarperBusiness Essentials.

———. 1954. *The Practice of Management*. New York: Harper and Row.

Friedman, Uri. 2020. "New Zealand's Prime Minister May Be the Most Effective Leader on the Planet." *The Atlantic*, April.

Freire, Paolo. 1970. *Pedagogy of the oppressed*. New York, NY: Continuum.

Fullan, Michael. 2014. *Change Leader: Learning to do What Matters Most*. San Francisco: Jossey-Bass Press, 2011.

———. 2003. *The Moral Imperative of School Leadership*. California: Corwin Press.

———. 2007. *The New Meaning of Educational Change*. New York: Teachers College Press.

———. 2014. *The Principal—Three Keys to Maximizing Impact*. San Francisco: Jossey-Bass Press.

Gibbons, Deborah E. 2004. "Friendship and Advice Networks in the Context of Changing Professional Values." *Administrative Science Quarterly* 49 (2): 238–62. SAGE Publishing. doi:10.2307/4131473.

Gilligan, Carol. 1982. *In a Different Voice*. Cambridge, MA: Harvard University Press.

Goleman, Daniel. 1998. *Working with emotional intelligence*. New York: Bantam Books.

Gruenewald, D. A. 2003. "The best of both worlds: A critical pedagogy of place." *Educational Researcher* 32(4): 3–12.

Hersey, Paul, and Kenneth H. Blanchard. 1982. "Leadership Style: Attitudes and Behaviors." *Training and Development Journal* 36 (5): 50–52.

Herzberg, Frederick. 1987 "One More Time: How do you Motivate Employees?" *Harvard Business Review* 65 (5): 109–20.

Hecht, Ben. 2014. "Collaboration Is the New Competition." *Harvard Business Review.* August 7. https://hbr.org/2013/01/collaboration-is-the-new-compe.

Heck, Ronald H., and Philip Hallinger. 2009. "Assessing the Contribution of Distributed Leadership to School Improvement and Growth in Math Achievement." *American Educational Research Journal* 46 (3): 659–89.

Hurley, Robert F. 2014. "The Decision to Trust." *Harvard Business Review.* August 21. https://hbr.org/2006/09/the-decision-to-trust.

Hutton, Disraeli M. 2011. "Revealing the Essential Characteristics, Qualities and Behaviours of the High Performing Principal: Experiences of the Jamaican School System." *International Journal of Educational Leadership Preparation* 5 (3): 1–15.

Hutton Disraeli M., and Beverley Johnson, eds. 2017. *Leadership for Success: The Jamaican School Experience.* The University of the West Indies Press.

Jackson, David. "Donald Trump Accepts GOP Nomination says 'I alone can fix' system." USA Today, July 21, 2016. https://www.usatoday.com/story/news/politics/elections/2016/07/21/donald-trump-republican-convention-acceptance-speech/87385658/ Accessed on April 16, 2020.

Janis, Irving L. 1982. *Groupthink.* Boston: Houghton Mifflin.

Juran, Joseph M. 2003. *Juran on Leadership for Quality: An Executive Handbook.* New York: Simon and Schuster.

Kellerman, Barbara. 2008. *Followership: How Followers are Creating Change and Changing Leaders.* Boston: Harvard Business School Press.

Kelley, Robert. 1992. *The Power of Followership.* New York: Bantam Doubleday Dell Publishing Group.

Kincheloe, J. L. 2005. *Critical Pedagogy Primer.* Switzerland: Peter Lang Publishing.

King, Martin Luther, Jr. "Why Can't We Wait." April 16, 1963, Birmingham, UK. https://www.africa.upenn.edu/Articles_Gen/Letter_Birmingham.html.

Kotter, John P. 1996. *Leading Change*. Cambridge, MA: Harvard Business School Press.

———. 2013. "Management Is (Still) Not Leadership." *Harvard Business Review*. March 29. https://hbr.org/2013/01/management-is-still-not-leadership.

Lagarde, Christine. 2019. "Angela Merkel – Striking the Right Note on Leadership." *International Monetary Fund,* August 31. https://www.imf.org/en/News/Articles/2019/08/31/sp083119-Angela-Merkel-Striking-the-Right-Note-on-Leadership.

"Leadership for the 21st Century: Chaos, Conflict, and Courage." 2024. *Harvard Kennedy School*. January 21. https://www.hks.harvard.edu/educational-programs/executive-education/leadership-21st-century.

Lebowitz, Shana. 2017. "16 Psychological Tricks to make people like us Immediately." *Independent Newspaper*, September 26. https://www.independent.co.uk/life-style/sixteen-psychological-tricks-people-you-a7967861.html.

Lehmann. Paul L. 2006. *Ethics in a Christian Context*. Kentucky: Westminster John Knox Press.

Leithwood, Kenneth, Alma Harris, and David Hopkins. 2008. "Seven Strong Claims About Successful School Leadership." *School Leadership and Management* 28 (1): 27–42.

Leman, Kevin, and William Pentak. 2004. *The Way of the Shepherd: Seven Secrets to Managing Productive People*. Grand Rapids, MI: Zondervan.

Mandela, Nelson. "State of the Nation Address." Speech, Cape Town, South Africa, May 24, 1994. South African History Online. https://www.sahistory.org.za/article/african-national-congress-anc.

Manley, Michael. 1975. *A Voice at the Workplace: Reflections on Colonialism and the Jamaican Worker*. Cambridge, MA: Howard University Press.

Martin, Roger. 2017. "The 3 Simple Rules of Managing Top Talent." *Harvard Business Review*, February 24. https://hbr.org/2017/02/the-3-simple-rules-of-managing-top-talent?autocomplete=true.

McClelland, David C. 1961. *The Achieving Society.* Princeton, N.J.: Van Nostrand.

McGregor, Douglas. 1960. *The Human Side of Enterprise.* New York: McGraw-Hill.

McInerney, Sarah. 2011. "Steve Jobs: An Unconventional Leader." *ExecutiveStyle,* October 7. http://www.executivestyle.com.au/steve-jobs-an-unconventional-leader-1lcmo.

Miller, William R., and Stephen Rollnick. 2012. *Motivational Interviewing: Helping People Change.* New York: Guilford Press.

Mills, Charles. 1997. *The Racial Contract.* Ithaca: Cornell University Press.

Mills-Schofield, Deborah. 2012. "Let's Bring Back Accountability." *Harvard Business Review,* July 30. https://hbr.org/2012/07/lets-bring-back-accountability.

Molm, Linda D. 2003. "Power, Trust and Fairness: Comparisons of Negotiated and Reciprocal Exchange." In *Power and Status (Advances in Group Processes, Volume 20),* edited by Shane R. Thye and John Skvoretz, 31–65. Bingley, UK: Emerald Group Publishing Limited.

Monarth, Harrison. 2014. "Make Your Team Feel Powerful." *Harvard Business Review,* May 7. https://hbr.org/2014/05/make-your-team-feel-powerful.

Murphy, Joseph, Michael Vriesenga, and Valerie Storey. 2007. "An Analysis of Types of Work, Methods of Investigation, and Influences." *Educational Administration Quarterly* 43 (5): 612–28.

Myatt, Mike. 2012. "Leadership, Influence and Relationships." *N2 Growth,* October 8. https://hub.n2growth.com/leadership-influence.

Noddings, Nel. 2003. *Caring: A Feminine Approach to Ethics and Moral Education.* University of California Press: Berkeley.

Nunnally, Jum C. 1978. *Psychometric Theory,* 2nd ed. New York: McGraw-Hill.

Ouchi, William. G. 1981. "The Z Organization". In *Classics of Organizational Theory,* 6th ed., edited by J.M. Shafritz, J.S. Ott, and J Y.S. Jang, 424–35. Belmont, CA: Wadsworth.

Peck, Morgan Scott. 1994. *A World Waiting to be Born: Civility Rediscovered.* New York: Bantam Doubleday Dell Publishing Group.

Peters, Kai and Matthew Gitsham. "Developing the Global Leader of Tomorrow." *EFMD Global Focus* 3 (1): 58–61.

Peters, Tom. 1987. *Thriving on Chaos.* New York: Harper and Row.

Petter, Olivia. 2018. "Millennials Set to be Outnumbered by Gen Z Within a Year." *Independent.* August 22. https://www.independent.co.uk/life-style/millennials-gen-z-outnumbered-2019-global-population-demographic-bloomberg-a8502251.html.

Piccolo, Ronald. 2005. "Transformational Leadership and Follower Risk Behaviour: An Examination of Framing and Issue Interpretation." PhD Dissertation. University of Florida. https://ufdc.ufl.edu/UFE0011465/00001/1x.

Popa, Ioan Lala, Gheorghe Preda, and Monica Boldea. 2010. "A Theoretical Approach of the Concept of Innovation." *Managerial Challenges of the Contemporary Society. Proceedings*, 151.

Rawls, John. 1972. *A Theory of Justice.* Oxford: Oxford University Press.

Rezaei, Morad, Sajjad Salehi, Masomeh Shafiei, and Somaye Sabet. 2012. "Servant Leadership and Organizational Trust: The Mediating Effect of the Leader Trust and Organizational Communication." *EMAJ: Emerging Markets Journal* 2 (1): 70–78.

Robinson, Jessica. 2021. "Leadership Lessons of the Highest Order from Angela Merkel." *Leaderonomics.com,* June 22. https://www.leaderonomics.com/articles/leadership/leadership-lessons-of-the-highest-order-from-angela-merkel-

Robinson, Nick. 2013, "Economy: There is no alternative (TINA) is back", March 07. https://www.bbc.com/news/uk-politics-21703018.

Ryan, James. 2006. "Inclusive Leadership and Social Justice for Schools." *Leadership and Policy in Schools* 5 (1): 3–17.

Scandura, Terri. A., and Monica Sharif. 2011."Leadership and Organizational Change." *Management Faculty Articles and Papers,* Paper 12.

Schriesheim, Chester, and Linda L. Neider. 2012. *Research in Management: Perspectives on Justice and Trust in Organizations.* IAP-Information Age Publishing, Incorporated.

Seidman, Gwendolyn. 2018. "Why Do We Like People Who Are Similar to Us?" December 18. https://www.psychologytoday.

com/us/blog/close-encounters/201812/why-do-we-people-who-are-similar-us.
Smith, Alan D. 2011. "Corporate Social Responsibility Implementation: Comparison of Large Not-For-Profit and For-Profit Companies." *International Journal of Accounting and Information Management* 19 (3): 231–46.
Spillane, James and Alma Harris. 2008. "Distributed leadership through the looking glass." *Management in Education* 22: 31–34. 10.1177/0892020607085623.
Taylor, Paul and George Gao. 2014. "Generation X: America's neglected 'middle child'." *Pew Research Centre*, June 5. https://www.pewresearch.org/short-reads/2014/06/05/generation-x-americas-neglected-middle-child/.
Thompson, Canute S. 2009. *Toward Solutions: Fundamentals of Transformational Leadership in a Post-Modern Era*. Mandeville: Northern Caribbean University Press.
———. 2013. *Leadership Reimagination: A Primer of Principles and Practices*. Kingston: Caribbean Leadership Reimagination Initiative.
———. 2017. "Teachers' Expectations of Educational Leaders' Leadership Approach and Perspectives on the Principalship: Identifying Critical Leadership Paradigms for the 21st Century." *Journal of Organizational and Educational Leadership* 2 (2): 4. https://digitalcommons.gardner-webb.edu/joel/vol2/iss2/4.
———. 2018a. "Leadership Behaviours that Nurture Organizational Trust: Re-Examining the Fundamentals." *Journal of Human Resource Management* 21 (1): 28–42.
———. 2018b. *Reflections on Leadership and Governance in Jamaica: Towards a Better Society*. Kingston: Arawak Publications.
———. 2019a. "Examining Teachers' Perspectives on Effective Organizational Change Strategies." *Educational Planning* 26 (2).
———. 2019b. *Reimagining Educational Leadership in the Caribbean*. Kingston: University of the West Indies Press.
———. 2020. *Education and Development: Policy Imperatives for Jamaica and the Caribbean*. Kingston: The University of the West Indies Press.

Thompson, Canute S., Sheron Burgess, and Thenjiwe Major. 2019. "Towards a Philosophy of Education for the Caribbean: Exploring African Models of Integrating Theory and Praxis." *Journal of Thought, Fall/Winter,* 53–72.

Thompson, Canute. S., Burke, Tabika, King, Kerry-Ann and Wong, Shelly-Ann. 2017. "Leadership Strategies for Turning Around Underperforming Schools: Lessons from Two Jamaican Schools." *Journal of Education and Development in the Caribbean* 16 (2): 28–42.

Thompson, Canute S., Glenda Prescod and Allison Montgomery. 2020. *An Exploration of Philosophical Assumptions that inform Educational Policy in Jamaica: Conversations with former and current Education Ministers.* Kingston: Arawak Publication.

Tracy, David. 1981. *The Analogical Imagination: Christian Theology and the Culture of Pluralism.* New York: Crossroad.

Vick, Karl. 2015. "Angela Merkel – Time Magazine's Person of the Year." *Insider,* December 9.

Wheatley, Margaret. 1999. *Leadership and the New Science: Discovering Order in a Chaotic World.* San Francisco: Berrett-Koehler.

White, Jessica. 2014. "Millennial Generation Eager to Work, 'But on Their Terms'." *The Columbus Dispatch,* March 30.

Wigglesworth, Robin. 2020. "Inside the IMF's Outrageous, Improbably Successful Jamaican Programme (Pt. 2)." February 17. https://www.ft.com/content/e1f0cf23-6a83-4c61-a880-d7984c5a8f6f.

Wilson, Suze. 2020. "Pandemic Leadership: Lessons from New Zealand's Approach to COVID-19." *Leadership* 16 (3).

Wood Jr, James Andy, and Bruce E. Winston. 2005. "Toward a New Understanding of Leader Accountability: Defining a Critical Construct." *Journal of Leadership and Organizational Studies,* 11 (3): 84–94.

World Bank. 2019. World Bank Update. October 7. Accessed from https://www.worldbank.org/en/country/jamaica/overview. April 16, 2020.

Yilmaz, Kürşad, and Yahya Altinkurt. 2012. "Relationship Between the Leadership Behaviors, Organizational Justice and Organizational Trust." *Çukurova University Faculty of Education Journal* 41 (1): 12.

Zenger, Jack and Joseph Folkman. 2020. "What Inspiring Leaders

Do." *Harvard Business Review*. January 9. https://hbr.org/2013/06/what-inspiring-leaders-do.

Zhang, Yenming, Tzu-Bin Lin, and Suan Fong Foo. 2012. "Servant Leadership: A Preferred Style of School Leadership in Singapore." *Chinese Management Studies* 6 (2): 369–83.

3M Company. "Company Profile, Information, Business Description, History, Background Information on 3M Company." *Reference for Business*. Last modified 2019. https://www.referenceforbusiness.com/history2/22/3M-Company.html.

Index

3M company (USA) 105–10

ABCD trust model 88
abundance mentality 38, 39
accountability 52, 53–9
Accra Agenda for Action 53
"advocate for justice" factor 19, *25*, 33, 83
African National Congress (ANC) 139
ajjava concept 7, 8–9
Alcoff, Linda Martin xxii
alienated followers/leaders 57
alternatives-thinking 33–5, 38, 93–4, 106–7, 113–14, 133, 141, 143
Altinkurt, Yahya 82–3
analogical imagination 13
Anthony, Scott D. 37
Apple Inc. 37
Ardern, Jacinda xx–xxi, 142
Aristotle 12–13

Barbados 140
Barret, Will 52
Barth, Karl xx, 136–7
benchmarking 13
Biggs, Dick 48–9
Bivins, Thomas 52
Black, Jan Kippers 64
Blanchard, Kenneth H. 57–8, 88

Blasé, Jo 84
Blasé, Joseph 84
Boyden World Corporation 36
Bromfield, Nicholas 143
Brown, Arthur 123
Brueggemann, Walter xxix, 3, 10–12, 16
Buddhism 7–9, 17
Burton, Brian K. 78
Byham, William 85

care 77–81
Carnegie, Dale 77
Cavanaugh, William 10
change catalysation 61–8
chaos theory 40–1, 62
character ethic 78
Charles, Jacqueline 112
Chile 10
Christensen, Clayton 108
Christianity
 see Judeo-Christian tradition
Chuang, Szufang 4–5
Clarke, Nigel 112, 114
Climate Conference (Glasgow 2021) 141
Cohen, Michael 14
Coke, Christopher 113
commoditization of knowledge 70–1
conformist followers/leaders 57
constructive subversion 65–8

Cooke, Howard 117
courage 61, 68–75, 97–8
Covey, Stephen R. 12, 38–9, 78
Covid-19 pandemic 111, 142
Craig, Geoffrey 143
critical pedagogy xviii–xxi
critical-thinking engagement 58

Damanpour, Fariborz 42
"demonstrate care" factor 19, 26, 33, 51, 77
departmental cooperation 109–10
Duncan, Donna 100, 101, 102, 103
Duncan, Joan 100
Dunn, Craig P. 78
Dussel, Enrique xxii

economic policy 111–16
Economic Programme Oversight Committee (EPOC) (Jamaica) 114, 130
education policy
  see schools, teachers
employee share ownership plans (ESOPs) 103
empowerment
  see people empowerment
Enlightenment 15
exemplary followers/leaders 57

Fayol, Henri 55
Folkman, Joseph 42, 83
Freire, Paulo xix
Friedman, Uri 142
Fullan, Michael 47, 84

General Motors 34
Generation X (Gen Xers) xxiii, xxiv, xxvii
Generation Y (Millennials) xxiii, xxiv, 19, 27, 86

Generation Z (Gen Z) xxiii–xxiv
Gilligan, Carol 78
global recession (2008) 111
Goleman, Daniel 14
groupthink 72
Gutfreund Intelligence (GI) Group xxiv, xxv, 29, 40, 42, 46

Harvard Kennedy School 5, 17
Hersey, Paul 57–8
Herzberg, Frederick xxv, 40
Humphrey, Hubert 64
Hus, Jan 135–6
Hutton, Disraeli M. 85, 115

IBM 36
influence/power 42–9, 109, 113–15
innovation 37, 107–8
inspiration 108
"interest in the opinions of staff" factor 19
International Monetary Fund (IMF) 111, 112, 113, 114–15, 123, 125, 126

Jamaica
  accountability of political leaders 54
  economic policy 111–16
  school principals 85
  schools 93–9
  teachers 18–27
Jamaica College 118
Jamaica Money Market Brokers (JMMB) 100–4
Janis, Irving L. 72
Jobs, Steve 37
Johnson, Beverley 115
Judeo-Christian tradition 10, 17
Juran, Joseph M. 46
justice 81–5

Kellerman, Barbara 58
Kelley, Robert 57
khanti concept 7, 9
Kifer, Yona 80, 84
King, Martin Luther, Jr xx, 66-7, 137-9
Kotter, John P 36, 61, 65

Lebowitz, Shana 14
Lehmann. Paul L. 52
Leman, Kevin 88, 89
Luther, Martin 136

maddava concept 7, 9
Manchester, Jamaica 116
Mandela, Nelson xx, 67, 139-40
Manley, Michael 46, 131
Manley, Thomas 117
McClelland, David C. xxv, 46
McConnell, Allan 143
McGregor, Douglas xxiv-xxv
McInerney, Sarah 37
meaningful inclusion 81-2
Miller, William R. 62
Mills, Charles xxii
Mills-Schofield, Deborah 52, 88-9
Ministry of Education, Jamaica 85
Monarth, Harrison 80, 84
Moore, Thomas xxii
Moravian church 135
Mottley, Mia xx, xxi, 140-2
mutual accountability 51-60, 100, 101-2, 103, 110
Myatt, Mike 44-6

negative influence 48
negotiation 48-9
Neider, Linda L. 82
New Zealand 142
Noddings, Nel 78

Oasis High school (pseudonym) 93, 94
Organization for Economic Cooperation and Development (OECD) 53
Ouchi, William. G. 46

Paradigm RePaDO 23, 35, 40, 46-7
Paris Declaration on Climate Change 53
Parks, Rosa xx, 133-4
parricaga concept 7, 8
passive followers/leaders 57
Peck, Scott 72
Pentak, William 88, 89
people empowerment 35-41, 106-7
People's National Party (Jamaica) 112
perseverance 73-5
personal accountability 54-6
Peters, Tom 40-1
Phillips, B. B. 117
Phillips, Peter 111-12, 113, 114, 115-16
  interview with author
  appointment as Minister of Finance 121-2
  background/childhood 116-19
  historical context 122-3
  leadership philosophy 131-3
  political ideology 120
  priorities 123-4
  trust deficit 125-31
Piccolo, Ronald 97
Poincare, Henri 62
power
  see influence/power
power-sharing 108-9
presidential election (USA 2012) 89
Proposition MRM 101

Rawls, John xxii, 12, 81–2
Reaganomics 41
risk-taking 63, 97–8
Rollnick, Stephen 62
Ryan, James 81–2

Scandura, Terri. A. 61
scarcity mentality 38–9
school principals 85
schools 93–9
  see also teachers
Schriesheim, Chester 82
Seaview High school (pseudonym) 93, 94, 95, 96, 98
Seidman, Gwendolyn 14
self-transcendence 59
Sharif, Monica 61
Sloan, Alfred 34
Socrates 13
solutions-orientation 101–2
South Africa 139
stock market crash (USA 1987) 41
subversion 63–4
succession planning 86–7

Taylor, Frederick 55
teachers 18–27
  see also schools

Thatcher, Margaret 37
Thompson, Canute S. xxii, 27, 46–7, 70, 93, 101–2, 115
Tracy, David 12–13
Trump, Donald 13–14, 77
Truss, Liz 37–8
trust 88–9, 97, 100, 101
trust deficit 112–13, 114, 125, 127–8
Turkey 82

"under-promise and over-deliver" maxim 54
United Kingdom 37–8
United States of America 11–12, 84

Watergate scandal 64
Wheatley, Margaret 40
Wigglesworth, Robin 112, 113
Wilson, Suze 143
World Bank 112
Wyclif, John 134–5
Wynter, Brian 112, 124

"yesmanship" 55–6
Yilmaz, Kürşad 82–3

Zenger, Jack 42, 83
Zhang, Yenming 84–5

www.ingramcontent.com/pod-product-compliance
Lightning Source LLC
Chambersburg PA
CBHW021142230426
43667CB00005B/221